Bureaucracy and
Statesmanship:
Henry Kissinger and the Making
of American Foreign Policy

THE CREDIBILITY OF INSTITUTIONS, POLICIES AND LEADERSHIP
A Series funded by the Hewlett Foundation
Kenneth W. Thompson, *Series Editor*

Bureaucracy and Statesmanship:

Henry Kissinger and the Making of American Foreign Policy

The Credibility of Institutions, Policies and Leadership

Volume 9

Robert J. Strong

Series Editor
Kenneth W. Thompson

University Press of America
Lanham • New York • London

The
White Burkett
Miller Center

Copyright © 1986 by

University Press of America,® Inc.

4720 Boston Way
Lanham, MD 20706

3 Henrietta Street
London WC2E 8LU England

Library of Congress Cataloging-in-Publication Data

Strong, Robert J. 1948-
    Bureaucracy and statesmanship.

    (The Credibility of institutions, policies and
leadership ; v. 9)
    Bibliography: p.
    1. Kissinger, Henry, 1923-   . 2. United States—
Foreign relations administration.   3. United States—
Foreign relations—1969-1974.   4. United States—Foreign
relations—1974-1977.   I. Title.   II. Series.
E840.8.K58S77 1986   327.73'0092'4   86-11055
ISBN 0-8191-5452-0 (alk. paper)
ISBN 0-8191-5453-9 (pbk. : alk. paper)

Co-published by arrangement with
The White Burkett Miller Center of Public Affairs,
University of Virginia

Acknowledgements

This book began as a doctoral dissertation and thus comes encumbered with all the debts that are acquired in graduate education. The dissertation was supervised by Professor Kenneth W. Thompson who provided constant encourgement and insightful criticism. The other members of my dissertation committee at the University of Virginia were Professors Carnes Lord, Inis Claude, Frederick Mosher and David Shannon.

Much of what is worthwhile in this work is a reflection of what I learned from some remarkable teachers of political science. Professors Robert Horwitz, Harry Clor, William Frame, Martin Diamond, and Morton Frisch gave me a thorough education in political theory and American political thought. Professors Mosher and Steven Rhoads taught me public administration, giving careful attention to the fundamental issues, as well as the practical applications, of that field. Professors Thompson and Claude at the University of Virginia, and Professor Lawrence Finkelstein at Northern Illinois University, introduced me to the serious study of international relations and encouraged me to bring to that study what I had learned in others areas of political science. Professor Herbert Storing, more than anyone else, gave me ideas about bureaucracy and statesmanship and an example of scholarship which I have imperfectly imitated.

My debts in the preparation of this book are intellectual rather than financial because of the generous support I received from the Institute for the Study of World Politics, the Woodrow Wilson Department of Government and Foreign Affairs, and the White Burkett Miller Center of Public Affairs at the University of

Virginia. In 1981–82 I also received an Earhart Fellowship which allowed me to begin extensive revisions of the dissertation in preparation for its publication as a book.

Portions of the revised manuscript were read by David Clinton and David Nichols who always had helpful corrections and useful suggestions.

To these institutions and individuals I owe more than I can properly acknowledge. I would only hope that I can partially repay their generous assistance by striving to achieve the high standards of teaching and research to which they are devoted.

To my wife, Elaine, my debts are greatest because the love and support she gives are given without thought of repayment.

Permission to reprint passages from the following books is gratefully acknowledged:

Henry A. Kissinger. *American Foreign Policy*, 3rd edition. New York: W. W. Norton, 1977.

Henry A. Kissinger. *White House Years*. Boston: Little Brown, 1979.

A revised version of chapter three in this book was previously published under the title "Kissinger: Statesmanship in a Bureaucratic Age," in Kenneth W. Thompson, editor. *Traditions and Values: American Diplomacy 1945 to the Present*. Lanham, Maryland: University Press of America, 1984.

Table of Contents

Preface
Kenneth W. Thompson

We are pleased to include a volume by Dr. Robert A. Strong in the Hewlett Series on the Credibility of Institutions and Leadership. Dr. Strong is an example of a new generation of scholars who are opening up new vistas of thought and inquiry in presidential studies and public affairs. He was a student of the late Herbert Storing, the first Director of Presidential Studies at the Miller Center. Subsequently, he assisted James Sterling Young in his research on the contemporary presidency. Now the two are embarking on a study of the Carter Presidency based on the oral history project on the Carter White House which Professsor Young has directed.

Robert Strong combines an early interest in political theory going back to the formative influence of the great political philosopher Leo Strauss on scholars such as Herbert Storing with a strong interest in foreign policy. What sets Strong apart from some equally outstanding younger theorists is his determination to put political theory to work. It is political theory applied to contemporary problems that characterizes Strong's approach. Not only does Strong display a firm grounding in classical political philosophy but he is also an authority on questions of armaments and arms control manifested in other writings. It is fitting that his book on bureaucracy be included with works on law, the private sector and the media as major institutions in American life.

Introduction

Few periods in the history of American foreign policy have elicited the range and intensity of comment and criticism that surround the years of Henry Kissinger's service in the White House and the State Department. While in office Kissinger was exuberantly praised in the media, even by those reporters and columnists who had rightfully earned their place on Nixon's various lists of enemies. For a time he was constantly on the cover of news magazines and in 1973 he became the first American Secretary of State to win a Nobel Peace Prize since George Marshall, and the first ever to do so for services rendered while a White House adviser. Though he served two presidents who had long political careers, he managed to garner a reputation that for a time exceeded either of his employers.

By 1976 this national and international adoration was waning. The approaching presidential election brought to the fore critics of both the substance and style of Kissinger's diplomacy in both political parties and on both sides of the ideological spectrum. The two administrations which have served in Washington since Kissinger's departure entered office promising to conduct American diplomacy in a manner that would mark a departure from the Kissinger era. Out of office for nearly a decade, Henry Kissinger continues to be surrounded by controversy as each new chapter in the history of the Nixon and Ford administrations emerges from the work of journalists, historians, archivists, and from Kissinger's own monumental memoirs. The wisdom of many of the policy initiatives in the Kissinger years is frequently debated; so are the methods used by Kissinger in formulating and pursuing those initiatives. Particularly in the first Nixon administration, but throughout his years in Washington, Kissinger dominated the foreign policy-making apparatus of the American government to an extent unprecedented and unduplicated in the postwar era. His ability to do this was a result of the particular conditions of the late 1960s and the personality traits of the presidents for whom he served. But it was also a conscious attempt to overcome bureaucratic lethargy in American foreign policy.

Every postwar president, scores of political observers and commentators, numerous commissions and committees, and a distinguished procession of academics have complained about the bureaucratic problem in American foreign policy. A minor school in the field of international relations is devoted to the study of bureaucratic politics, and proposing reforms for the organizations responsible for the conduct of American foreign affairs has become a cottage industry in our nation's capital. One of the reforms frequently proposed is the centralization of power in the White House and the dominance of the bureaucracies by an activist president. Enthusiasm for this solution often depends on what policies are being pursued and which president is being active, but centralization of foreign policymaking power in the White House remains a logical response to a bureaucratic policymaking structure thought to be disloyal or ineffective. From 1969 to 1975 Henry Kissinger exercised personal control over American foreign policy which rendered much of the bureaucracy irrelevant and contributed to the controversy surrounding his legacy.

This study will not attempt to provide a comprehensive evaluation of Kissinger's policies and performance. Instead it focuses on the relationship between the White House and the permanent organizations responsible for American foreign policy during the Kissinger era, and the broader issues raised for modern statesmen by the existence of large bureaucracies. It begins by looking at the bureaucratic problem in American foreign policy. For most observers any discussion of bureaucracy and foreign policy assumes the existence of a problem and explicitly or implicitly proposes a solution. Unfortunately, the descriptions of the bureaucratic problem are not always consistent and the reforms proposed, and sometimes enacted, in the last few decades have reflected those inconsistencies.

Not all observers regard the bureaucratic nature of our policymaking organizations as a problem capable of solution and many analysts, particularly those who study bureaucratic politics, urge political leaders to understand and accept the bureaucratic environment in which they must unavoidably operate. In chapter two the models of bureaucratic politics popular in studies of American foreign policy are discussed. According to these models, bureaucrats and presidents will constantly compete in a game that neither can fully win, and policy will always be made by the bargaining between politicians and bureaucrats. That bargaining constitutes the essence of foreign policymaking, and good policy requires the coincidence of an individual who advocates wise policies and has the bureaucratic skills to impose them on the chaos which normally prevails.

For both the observers of foreign policymaking in Washington and the theorists of bureaucratic politics, the bureaucratic problem involves the way large organizations process information, outline options, and implement decisions. The solution, to the extent that there is one, is a matter of understanding the true nature of policymaking and marginally improving performance with modest reforms. There is, however, another account of the bureaucratic problem that differs from the conventional wisdom and academic models that dominate most discussions of this subject. Chapter three examines Kissinger's treatment of the bureaucratic problem in the books and articles he wrote before going to Washington. The relationship between statesmanship and bureaucracy is a constant theme in Kissinger's writing about both nineteenth and twentieth century international affairs and it shares a great deal with the classic treatment of this subject provided by Max Weber. For both Weber and Kissinger the bureaucratic problem is not a tension or competition between leaders and bureaucrats, but the tendency of a bureaucratic age to fail to produce individuals with genuine leadership qualities. The rise of bureaucracies coincides with the decline of statesmen and only accidents of personality or history will enable creative individuals to exercise leadership in a bureaucratic age, and their ability to do so will always be temporary. Weber's familiar description of leadership emphasizes the importance of personality and the power of charisma;

Kissinger's leader is the rare individual possessing a sense of history, a vision of the future, and the ability to manipulate events sufficiently to produce a more stable world order. Both see leadership being stifled in our century with disastrous consequences for international relations.

Kissinger's criticisms of American foreign policymaking in the postwar era and his observations about the relationship between bureaucracies and statesmen raise interesting questions about the status of his own stewardship of American foreign policy. Was Kissinger merely a successful bureaucratic politician who was able to maximize his personal power at the expense of the Secretary of State and the permanent bureaucracies? Or was he something more? Was he a statesman manipulating the bureaucracy for a larger purpose? Does Kissinger's style of dealing with the foreign policy organizations of the government constitute a viable response to the bureaucratic problem in American foreign policy, or does it involve too many costs: is it a treatment that is worse than the disease it was intended to cure? These questions are addressed in the fourth and fifth chapters which deal with Kissinger's years in public office.

The central question, which for many readers will remain unresolved, is whether American foreign policy can be conducted without the inefficiencies inherent in complex organizations or the abuses that may occur when power is concentrated in the hands of a single leader. In a sense this is the central question for the American political regime which was founded by individuals who wanted to avoid both the inefficiencies of the Articles of Confederation and the abuses of George III. Raising this fundamental question does not resolve the controversy surrounding Henry Kissinger, but it may put that controversy in its most important context.

ONE

The Bureaucratic Problem In American Foreign Policy

There are few things about which most of the residents of Washington, D.C. agree. Beyond the facts that real estate prices are too high, summers too hot, and traffic circles too confusing, about the only opinion widely shared in our nation's capital is that something should be done about the foreign affairs bureaucracies. Even in a city of bureaucrats there is a general recognition that there are problems with the organizations that make and administer foreign policy. Whether they work in the agencies and departments of the federal government, in the Congress, in the media, or in the White House, participants and observers of politics in Washington almost universally criticize the size, the character, or the behavior of the permanent organizations responsible for foreign affairs. Such criticisms have been consistently made throughout the postwar era. Presidents, congressional committees, independent commissions, scholars and journalists have all reported problems in the management of foreign affairs. According to a leading scholar in this field there were eleven major studies of the organizations responsible for foreign affairs between 1945 and 1972.[1] There have been more since then. Unfortunately, even after all of this analysis, no one can be quite sure exactly what the bureaucratic problem in American foreign policy is. It is not that we know too little about this subject; it may be that we know too much.

Competing and sometimes contradictory theories explain bureaucratic behavior and attribute policy failures to various organizational dysfunctions. These theories and explanations

1

sometimes focus attention on how agencies and departments are organized, sometimes deal with the personnel who work in the executive branch, and sometimes emphasize the relationships between White House staff and civil servants. In every case there is good reason to expect problems in the conduct of foreign policy, and some hope that modest reforms will mitigate, if not eliminate, these problems. But what is true for each of the individual studies of bureaucracy and foreign policy is not true for all the studies taken together. In American foreign policy it is not at all clear what the bureaucratic problem is or what should be done about it. This seems to be an instance where the sum of the parts is considerably less than each isolated component.

The catalogue of complaints about American foreign policy bureaucracies is a long and varied one, but can be divided into a few broad categories.

CUMBERSOME BUREAUCRACY

Every president since Franklin Roosevelt has complained about the organizations that are supposed to carry out his military and foreign policies. Roosevelt reportedly told an associate that "to change anything in the Na-a-vy is like punching a feather bed," when you are finished punching, "you find the damn bed just as it was before you started punching."[2] Kennedy, according to the account given by his brother, was surprised to discover in the midst of the Cuban missile crisis that the American medium range missiles in Turkey, which he had ordered removed, were still in place. "The President believed he was President and that, his wishes having been made clear, they would be followed."[3] Truman said of his successor that when sitting in the Oval Office, "He'll say, 'Do this! Do that!' And nothing will happen. Poor Ike—it won't be a bit like the Army. He'll find it very frustrating."[4] It is not clear whether this anecdote demonstrates Truman's evaluation of Eisenhower's political naïveté or Truman's own misconceptions about the efficiency of the military. It probably shows both. All of the postwar presidents, but especially Johnson and Nixon, have been distressed by leaks of military and diplomatic information, and by their inability to find the sources of significant security breaches.

In all of these presidential observations there is a sense that the elected leader and the permanent employee of the government are natural enemies and that the federal government as a whole, and the national security organizations which are part of it, are unmanageable. Presidential suspicions seem to be highest when an election brings a new party into office, and when presidents and their appointees depend, more than usual, on civil servants. If it is somewhat exaggerated to think of politicians and bureaucrats as perpetual adversaries, it can at least be said that all of the chief executives in the last forty years have sometimes found the foreign policy organizations of the government to be slow, unresponsive, and difficult to change and coordinate. The national security bureaucracies are, if nothing else, cumbersome.

Part of the problem is simply size. Ever since the Hoover Commission Report of 1949, official studies and individual observers have agreed that there are too many organizations dealing with foreign policy and that many of them are too large. In 1978 there were sixty-two separate departments, agencies, and offices in the federal government dealing with one aspect or another of international affairs.[5] No single cabinet secretary is responsible for all of these organizations and the authority of ambassadors overseas has often been undermined by the existence of personnel and policies which are outside of State Department control. In addition to the fact that there are too many separate organizations having an impact on foreign affairs, many of those organizations are themselves so large and diverse that they act without coherent direction. The Department of Defense, even under the leadership of Robert McNamara, rarely gave the appearance of being a unified organization. It has always been subject to internal conflict between its military and civilian components and among the three service branches. The services, themselves, have difficulty acting with a single purpose because the various specialities within each service compete for limited funds and personnel. The State Department, according to a White House report written in the mid-1960s, is no more coherent than Defense. Organized along both regional and functional lines the State Department seemed to be, from a White House perspective, "a constellation of small power centers—some moving, some standing, some competing, some hiding, some growing, some decaying, a few coalescing, but more breaking apart into smaller fragments which soon develop all the organs and physiology of their parents."[6]

If the existence of too many organizations involved in foreign affairs makes the bureaucracy cumbersome, so does the related problem that many of those organizations employ too many people. One former ambassador claims that his embassy worked best when, as a result of local tensions, half the embassy staff was sent home.[7] A subcommittee of the Senate Committee on Government Operations chaired by Senator Henry Jackson, which conducted an extensive study of the foreign affairs bureaucracies in the mid-1950s, concluded that successful national security policymaking was inhibited by excessive staffing. "Unnecessary people make for unnecessary layering, unnecessary clearances and concurrences, and unnecessary intrusions on the time of officials working on problems of real importance. Many offices have reached and passed the point where the quantity of staff reduces the quality of the product."[8] Many critics of the State Department and Defense Department have proposed radical reductions in the number of people and levels of command that are involved in policy decisions. The Fitzshugh Report on defense reorganization in 1969 suggested that 30% of the personnel assigned to the headquarters of the Army, Navy and Air Force departments could easily be reassigned.[9] Smith Simpson, a former Foreign Service officer, suggests that the ranks of the State Department should be cut in half at the same time he recommends that the responsibilities of State be increased.[10] The expectation that the State Department could easily do more work with fewer people is indicative of how serious the consequences of over-staffing are thought to be.

Because the organizations responsible for foreign affairs are large and fragmented the problem of policy coordination becomes a massive one, and the solution usually involves the formation of formal or informal interagency groups. The proliferation of committees intended to give direction and coherence to the various elements of the government dealing with foreign affairs and national security ends up, however, making the delays and indecisiveness that presidents and analysts have found in the foreign policy bureaucracies even worse. Robert Lovett observed in his testimony before the Jackson subcommittee that in the Department of Defense "the constant increase in the number of committees—other than those statutorily created—has reached a point where they are no longer mere nuisances but have become positive menaces to the prompt and orderly conduct of business." Speaking more generally about committees in government which he referred to as that "glutinous mass of lonely men," Lovett argued that committees were inherently unable to provide the kind of direction that was needed in foreign affairs. The "derogation of the authority of the individual in government, and the exaltation of the anonymous mass, has resulted in a noticeable lack of decisiveness. Committees cannot effectively replace the decisionmaking power of the individual who takes the oath of office; nor can committees provide the essential qualities of leadership."[11] Beyond the fact that committees are incapable of exercising authority and leadership, they tend to produce reports and judgments which are diluted to reflect consensus or majority opinions. Speaking for the critics of the national security organizations, George F. Kennan points out that "thought is, by its very nature, an individual process, not a collective one; that to be useful thought must be communicated; that to be communicated it must be passed through the filter of the single mind that puts it into words; that it cannot, therefore, be greater than what a single mind can comprehend and state."[12] The fact that bureaucratic reports and recommendations often go through numerous clearances and committees means that those reports and recommendations will tend to be diluted, generalized and uncontroversial, frequently failing to serve the needs of decisionmakers.

Those who find the foreign policy bureaucracies cumbersome have no single explanation of how they got that way. There are a number of half humorous propositions and laws that purport to explain the pervasive dissatisfaction of presidents and analysts with the organization of foreign affairs. Richard Holbrooke, a Foreign Service officer, has proposed a corollary to Parkinson's Law concerning organizational growth: "The chances of catastrophe grow as organizations grow in number and size, and as internal communications become more time-consuming and less intelligible."[13] The root cause of the bureaucratic problem in foreign policy is often seen as the rapid and uncontrolled growth of the organizations dealing with national security after the

Second World War. A nation unaccustomed to international responsibility over-built and over-staffed its foreign policy organizations as a natural response to unknown problems and an uncertain future.

Charles Frankel claimed to have discovered several fundamental laws of bureaucracy while he served as Assistant Secretary of State for Education and Cultural Affairs: "Whatever happens in government could have happened differently, and it usually would have been better if it had.... Once things have happened, no matter how accidentally, they will be regarded as manifestations of an unchangeable Higher Reason."[14] The serious half of Frankel's observation is that organizations and policies often created quickly and haphazardly, become exceedingly hard to change.

Critics of the American foreign policy organizations often argue that the bureaucracies were once reasonably effective, but have lost their relevance in a changing world. They point to times and places when things worked well—Kennan in charge of the Policy Planning Staff, McNamara as Secretary of Defense, Marshall and Acheson in command of a State Department trusted by President Truman. The bureaucratic problem, in this account, goes through cycles of reform, degeneration and more reform. Organizations appropriate for waging the Second World War were not able to conduct a Cold War. The departments and agencies created during the Cold War became, in turn, obsolete as a new agenda of international problems emerged in the 1960s and 1970s.[15] The fact that organizations become outmoded may partially explain why they are also too large and diffuse. During periods of reform it may have been easier to create new agencies and new staff positions than to eliminate or change old ones. This was especially true for Franklin Roosevelt who made a conscious practice of ignoring established elements of the federal government, preferring to create formal or informal organizations to work around them.[16] If this procedure is practiced for very long the problems of bureaucratic coordination obviously get worse.

Though the critics who find the foreign policy organizations cumbersome admit that bureaucracies are difficult to change, they usually suggest reforms which they believe would improve the making and implementing of foreign policy. These suggestions may be more or less politically realistic, but they all involve some reorganization, some reduction or redistribution of personnel, and careful adherence to various principles of sound administration—uniting authority and responsibility, eliminating overlaps and over-staffing, centralizing power, or creating organizations in tune with existing international realities. It is no doubt true that some reformers overstate the case for particular proposals. As Harold Seidman has observed:

> The quest for coordination is in many respects the twentieth-century equivalent of the medieval search for the philosopher's stone. If only we can find the right formula for coordination, we can reconcile the irreconcilable, harmonize competing and wholly divergent interests, overcome irrationalities in our government structures, and make hard policy choices to which no one will dissent.[17]

While perfect coordination may be impossible, and the danger exists that the benefits of proposed reforms will be exaggerated, many observers feel that the cumbersome bureaucracy can be helped. Though the size and number of organizations needed to conduct American international relations will always present problems of coordination and responsiveness, these problems are not beyond partial remedy. Not everyone, however, sees the foreign affairs and national security bureaucracies as simply cumbersome. Some people see a more sinister and serious problem.

UNCHECKED BUREAUCRACY

For several decades, but particularly during the Vietnam War, some of the critics of the foreign policy bureaucracies have described these organizations as independent and powerful entities that make political decisions and control political leaders, rather than merely inhibiting political direction. The term "military-industrial complex" came to mean several things after it was coined by President Eisenhower, but for Eisenhower and many others who used those words, they referred to the extent to which bureaucrats and technical experts were pre-empting the role of elected officials. While the cumbersome bureaucracy was slow, indecisive, and likely to frustrate politicians, the unchecked bureaucracy was apt to act too quickly, with a clear and sometimes dangerous plan of operation, and with the conscious or manipulated consent of the Congress and the president. "We have learned," wrote John Kenneth Galbraith from our experiences in Vietnam, "that an overseas bureaucracy, once in existence, develops a life and purpose of its own. Control by Washington is exiguous. Control by the Congress is for practical purposes nonexistent."[18]

Two explanations are generally given for the rise of un-controlled bureaucratic power in the conduct of American foreign policy. First, the character of foreign policy problems, particularly those related to weapon development and military strategy, have become highly technical and, therefore, the experts lodged in the bureaucratic organizations of the government have become increasingly influential. The ideal of having political judgment exercised on the basis of expert advice can rarely be achieved because the technical and political aspects of many problems easily become intertwined. A recent Secretary of the Navy has complained that: "One of the most frustrating things I have encountered in this job has been a tendency on the part of some staff people to use systems analysis as a cover for what is really subjective judgment."[19] Of course, as long as appointed and elected officials realize that subjective judgments are hidden in technical reports, the extent of bureaucratic power can be limited. But many politicians, it is claimed, do not realize until it is too late that their decisions have been based on biased information. This is especially true in areas of national security where documents are classified and discussions of alternative courses of action are limited. It is frequently suggested that failures in American national security policy have occurred because intelligence agencies exaggerate the Soviet threat, because Pentagon planners project excessive needs for new weapon systems, and because military commanders in the field make overly-optimistic reports.[20] In each of these cases it would be difficult to challenge the information of those who have specialized or first-hand knowledge. A frustrated President Kennedy complained after the

Bay of Pigs, "All my life I have known better than to depend on the experts. How could I have been so stupid."[21]

The second explanation for the excessive and dangerous power of bureaucracy in foreign affairs involves the displacement of public policy goals by organizational interests and objectives. Bureaucracies are thought to be "cumbersome," as we saw, because they often become outmoded and out of step with a changing world environment. Here bureaucracies are thought to be "unchecked" because they consciously abandon the goals they were established to achieve in favor of self-generated and self-serving purposes. "Bureaucracies," Richard Barnet argues, "respond to their own inner logic and to their own laws. Bureaucracies lose touch with the original purposes for which they are founded, and bureaucratic momentum often carries men far beyond the point to which they originally intend to go."[22] Ironically, and somewhat confusingly, Barnet uses the terms "bureaucratic momentum" and "bureaucratic inertia" to refer to the same phenomena.[23] In the first phrase he means that, once created and set in motion, organizations have a life of their own; in the second phase he refers to the resistance of bureaucracies to public control. Both result in unchecked bureaucracy. Galbraith concurs, pointing out that "the tendency of bureaucracy to find purpose in whatever it is doing is superbly revealed by the experience of the past decade in Vietnam."[24] American involvement in Southeast Asia, Galbraith claims, continued long after the original reasons for intervention had lost credence. The bureaucracies, and especially the military ones, invented reasons for their action and clung to discredited arguments regardless of prevailing political opinions.

Not only do bureaucracies pursue policy objectives much further and longer than political leaders would desire, but in the worst cases they convert organizational interests into public goals. Those who see an unchecked bureaucracy in the midst of American foreign policy formation suggest that bureaucracies distort and pervert the political search for policies that will meet the national interest. Bureaucracies gather information and make recommendations to political leaders, and those recommendations may be based largely, or entirely, on organizational interests.

> The most pathological possibility presented by the
> ability of bureaucratic organizations to define the
> options open to policy-makers is that organizational
> interests will come in time to transcend national
> interests, and that executive agencies will force the
> adoption of policies which reflect, not the needs and
> interests of the country, but their own appetite for
> power, prestige, or security.[25]

For some analysts this tendency of bureaucracies to substitute
parochial agency preferences for national political goals is the
understandable consequence of dedicated military personnel
and civil servants honestly believing that the preservation of their
organization and the performance of their function are essential
to the nation. For the bureaucracy's more severe critics, the
problem of goal substitution has its roots in crass efforts by
organization members to protect their salaries, budgets, and
prerogatives.

In either case these distortions will not be a serious problem if
political leaders are aware of them and able to read department
reports and agency recommendations with an appropriate
amount of skepticism. But the critics of unchecked bureaucracy
usually argue that politicians often fail to distinguish between
what is good for particular organizations and what is good for the
nation. Many of the Vietnam War critics assert that America's
willingness to intervene in Southeast Asia was enhanced by the
existence of newly created counterinsurgency forces that were
eager to demonstrate their effectiveness. The creation of new
organizational capabilities also created powerful political
pressures for their use.[26] Admiral Leahy, military adviser to
Presidents Roosevelt and Truman, writes in his memoirs that
some of the Manhattan Project executives wanted the atomic
bomb to be used in Japan in order to justify their vast wartime
expenditures.[27] There is, in fact, little evidence that this was an
important consideration in the Hiroshima decision, but it is
significant that even in one of the most important presidential
decisions of this century a White House adviser could see
organizational budget interests at the heart of recommendations
made to the president. Bureaucracies, sometimes obviously,
sometimes subtly, impose their perspectives and interests on the

decisions of political leaders and those bureaucracies are unchecked because there are no guarantees that their biased recommendations will not become public policy.

Those who criticize the "cumbersome" bureaucracy have confidence that the bureaucratic problem, or at least its most serious manifestations, can be resolved by appropriate reforms within the executive branch. The critics who see an "unchecked" bureaucracy have to propose more radical changes. In order to detect and reject the biased information of experts, congressional and public access to executive branch decisionmaking must be opened up, and competing centers of expertise must be established in the White House, on the Hill, and among concerned citizens. In order to make sure that organizational interests, and particularly those of the military, do not dominate the policy process, the independence, the budgets, and the discretion of those organizations whose actions have proved to be unpopular must be attacked. In one sense, the problem of the unchecked bureaucracy is the weakness of political representatives confronted with expert advice and organizationally produced recommendations, the solution is a heavy dose of democracy that decentralizes experts and organizations and at the same time forces them to convince much larger numbers of people that they are indeed working for the national interest.

All of these proposals to correct unchecked bureaucracy would, obviously, tend to make the conduct of foreign policy more cumbersome. The two definitions of the bureaucratic problem and their respective reforms are almost totally incompatible. One group would centralize authority and responsibility; the other would disperse them. One group would streamline the policymaking process; the other would add new safeguards and new complications. One group would put its trust in the professionally trained soldiers and diplomats and in the officials, elected and appointed, who lead them; the other would trust, in the final analysis, only the people. The two groups could hardly be thinking about the same problem.

TIMID BUREAUCRACY

Not all the criticisms of the foreign affairs bureaucracies focus on organizational problems like size, complexity, and distribution of responsibility, or on political problems like maintaining democratic control of technically proficient independent agencies. Much of the literature dealing with the bureaucratic problem in foreign policy focuses on the short-comings of the particular bureaucrats employed in the American foreign policy agencies, and not with the ways they are organized or their interactions with political leaders. "Organization," Dean Rusk told an audience of Foreign Service officers, "seldom stands in the way of good people and seldom converts mediocrity into excellent performance."[28]

Most of the complaints about the quality of personnel responsible for foreign affairs involve the State Department which, according to one academic observer, is surpassed only by the Mafia in its low public reputation. The Mafia, however, gets its bad press from the fact that it "seems to work too well, whereas there are persistent doubts that the State Department works at all."[29] Explanations for the perceived poor performance of State Department employees vary widely and a series of postwar Foreign Service reforms have done little to reduce the number of complaints that policymakers and the public make about the department's personnel. Some of these complaints are extremely vague: "Somewhere there exists in the State Department a zone, or a climate, or inertia, which prevents it from thinking in terms of a new kind of politics, new departures in technique, an inertia which binds it rigidly to the fossil routines of conferences, negotiations, frozen positions."[30] It is not at all clear what a "zone" or a "climate" have to do with inertia, but it is often argued that the slowness of State Department responses to political instruction is caused by more than just size and decentralization and more than the frequently observed organizational resistance to change. State's inertia, according to some observers, is deeper and has its fullest explanation in the kind of people the organization recruits and promotes.

The Foreign Service is a highly selective, highly competitive, personnel system established by special legislation, and governed by its own personnel policies and rules. In the last four decades the service has produced a number of distinguished diplomats, and while most critics of State Department personnel policies acknowledge that America has had some effective negotiators and policy planners, they argue that these people have succeeded despite the Foreign Service rather than because of it. Ironically, the problem with the State Department bureaucracy is often related to the fact that it is extremely selective and competitive. Because existing Foreign Service officers have considerable leeway in deciding who enters and who rises in the organization, they end up, according to one critic, practicing a kind of "cloning."[31] The State Department remains conservative, resists change, avoids responsibility, and opposes bold action because it is run by a group of people lacking initiative and slow to perceive a rapidly evolving world. Although that is too sweeping a generalization and could not be supported by the facts, it represents the thrust of many of the criticisms of the Foreign Service. That system, it is claimed, both produces and perpetuates these traits.

Individuals joining and succeeding in the Foreign Service must do so by impressing their superiors and consistently receiving favorable performance evaluations. Because the number of senior positions, and especially ambassadorships, is rather small and because the number of people hoping to get those positions is relatively large, almost any blemish in a personnel file can have a significant impact on a diplomatic career. As a result of this competitiveness a number of things are thought to occur. According to at least one study, many promising young Foreign Service officers leave the State Department because the prospects for advancement are poor, because the period of apprenticeship required before gaining access to policymaking positions is unusually long, and because the constant pressure to satisfy supervisors and conform with their values is stifling.[32] More importantly, those who stay tend to be individuals comfortable in a career that involves a great deal of routine work in its early years, and gives deference to its most senior, and not necessarily its most able, members.

One former Foreign Service officer, William A. Bell, has written that "direct argument with one's superiors in State is not a generally accepted mode of conduct."[32] While serving in the Dominican Republic in 1965 Bell recalls that his ambassador gathered the embassy staff and informed them of the impending marine invasion and of its dubious public justification. The ambassador then asked for comments and criticisms; there were none. Chris Argyris, who has surveyed and interviewed Foreign

Service officers, concludes that they are "individuals who fear taking initiative" characterized by "withdrawal from interpersonal difficulties and conflict; minimum interpersonal openness; mistrust of others' aggressiveness; and withdrawal from aggressiveness and fighting."[33] It is by no means certain that aggressive diplomats would be preferable to nonaggressive ones, but the lack of initiative that Bell saw in his personal experience and Argyris discovered through his research has been observed by others. Arthur Schlesinger, writing about his days in the White House, "almost concluded that the definition of a Foreign Service officer was a man for whom the risks always outweighed the opportunities."[34] Dean Rusk, shortly after becoming Secretary of State, told a new class of Foreign Service officers: "There are those who think that the heart of a bureaucracy is a struggle for power. This is not the case at all. The heart of the bureaucratic problem is the inclination to avoid responsibilty."[35]

If timid bureaucrats are selected by a competitive and insular personnel system, they are also produced by the work that Foreign Service officers are called upon to perform. Trained to negotiate, ordered to be intransigent, assigned to study complicated problems that have remained unresolved for years, and, in an era of rapid world-wide communication, asked to refer all important matters to Washington, diplomats could easily conclude that initiative is not part of their job description. The harassment of Foreign Service officers during the McCarthy era could only have added to this tendency to act cautiously. The problem is that the successful diplomat conducting a tedious negotiation, or dealing with an insoluble international problem, or avoiding congressional attacks, may not be the best individual to act as a policy planner or as an adviser to politicians and political appointees who want to make dramatic changes in world affairs. John Leacacos, a diplomatic correspondent for several decades, noticed this incompatibility between the foreign and domestic demands on State Department employees. Pointing out that good diplomats abroad can be bad policymakers in Washington, Leacacos observed:

> The Foreign Service officer, habituated to bargain, negotiate and outsmart foreigners overseas, found it difficult not to handle his colleagues at home the same

way. The mentality at times appeared to be that of insurance agents. Everybody analyzed everything to death, and did nothing about it, or very little. The emphasis on emotional stability and control of temper tended to emasculate the spirited. The drilled habit of obeying orders inhibited imagination and daring.[36]

In addition to the fact that experience in foreign negotiations may not be appropriate training for Washington policymakers, it has frequently been argued that long service overseas makes it difficult for our diplomats to understand and advance American interests. This is not a new problem. When Jefferson was Secretary of State he suggested that agents of the American government serving abroad should be replaced every seven years.

I think it possible that it will be established into a maxim of the new government to discontinue its foreign servants after a certain time of absence from their own country, because they lose in time that sufficient degree of intimacy with its circumstances which alone can enable them to know and pursue its interests.[37]

Even when diplomats have not been overseas for seven years and have not lost touch with American society, they often become too sympathetic toward the foreign governments with which they deal. One State Department critic refers to this as "clientitus," a disease which affects the organs of perception and makes it likely that American diplomats will support the status quo and fail to anticipate revolutionary change.[38] Foreign Service officers, as well as intelligence and military personnel stationed overseas, are usually in close contact with the government officials of their host country. They may gather evidence, file reports, and make recommendations based on what they learn from these sources. As a result, Washington decisionmakers are told that the morale of the South Vietnamese army is high, that the Shah of Iran leads a stable regime, and that the National Guard in Nicaragua will be difficult to defeat. Mistakes in the interpretation of ambiguous foreign situations are to be expected, but the mistakes of American analysts, and particularly those in the State Department, appear to some observers to be systematic errors that reflect excessive contacts with existing authorities.[39]

To avoid or minimize the problems that accompany service overseas, the State Department frequently rotates its Foreign Service officers between the United States and foreign assignments and encourages officers to serve in a variety of countries and, sometimes in a variety of international regions. The object of this career pattern is to produce generalists who understand the complexity of the world and its problems. Unfortunately, to the extent that this policy succeeds, it tends to raise issues for a new set of State Department critics. While some observers of the foreign policy bureaucracies explain that the State Department lacks initiative and imagination because Foreign Service officers are too attached to the nations in which they serve, others argue that the department fails to come up with accurate projections or new policies because it has too many generalists and not enough specialists. Because very few policymakers or their advisers understood the history of Southeast Asia and the fact that the Chinese and Vietnamese were traditional enemies, it is argued, they overestimated the danger of Chinese intervention in behalf of Ho Chi Minh.[40] The State Department either lacks experts knowledgeable about some countries and regions or assigns the experts it has to jobs that fail to utilize this personnel resource. In addition to misusing or not developing regional experts, it is frequently observed that the State Department has "too little expertise in military, economic, and technical subjects, and too little capacity to plan or forecast."[41] Of course, should the State Department attempt to recruit and train more specialists, its bureaucracy might become less timid at the same time it became more cumbersome and more unchecked.

ELITIST BUREAUCRATS

The controversy surrounding the Foreign Service and the debates about whether it recruits and produces the right kind of diplomats and policymakers has another dimension. Rather than looking at the personnel policies of the State Department and asking how they affect the making of American foreign policy, many critics of the foreign affairs bureaucracies point to the social and economic backgrounds of those who serve and lead the national security organizations. The bureaucratic problem, they argue, is that American foreign policy is dominated by individuals whose economic interests, class origins, or shared attitudes prevent the government of the United States from perceiving and pursuing the true national interest. Whether the leaders of the foreign policy bureaucracies are part of an amorphous "establishment," a genuine economic conspiracy, or something in between is vigorously debated among these critics, but all agree that at least part of the problem with American foreign policy is that our bureaucrats are elitist.

Some observers regard senior military officers as the most important elite in the making of American foreign policy and argue that the close relationship between large corporations and the military explains the arms race and American imperialism.[42] Others focus their attention on the State Department and on the senior civil servants and politically appointed officials who hold foreign policymaking positions throughout the government. These people, despite significant exceptions, tend to have similar backgrounds—born to wealth, well educated in private schools and Ivy League colleges, often serving in government for brief periods during the course of legal, banking, or corporate careers. After studying the professional experience of senior foreign policymakers, Gabriel Kolko concluded:

> The foreign policy decision-makers are in reality a highly mobile sector of the American corporate structure.... A small number of men fill the large majority of key foreign policy posts. Their many diverse posts make this group a kind of committee government entrusted to handle numerous and varied national security and international functions at the policy level. Even if not initially connected with the corporate sector, career government officials relate in some tangible manner with the private worlds predominantly of big law, big finance, and big business.[43]

Kolko does not suggest that these individuals are engaged in a conscious scheme to promote private or corporate interests.

Instead, their presence in high office insures that a prevailing ideology supporting American military and economic dominance of the world will be the basis for all policy decisions.

The bureaucracy, according to the theorists of American elitism, is an arena for conspiracy or an instrument through which established economic and political ideas are given expression. In either case bureaucracies are less important than the bureaucrats who run them and the actions of those bureaucrats have their explanations outside the organizational character of the federal government. "Bureaucratic structures are less the source of power than the means by which others direct power in America for predetermined purposes."[44] Those who see economic or class interests at the root of America foreign policy do not consider bureaucracy, itself, to be a serious problem. Other critics of American foreign policy, however, describe a more subtle form of elitism that is created and reinforced by bureaucratic organizations.

The individuals who rise to the top of bureaucratic hierarchies often share common assumptions, attitudes, and experiences which make them just as much of an elite as would shared social or educational backgrounds. Martin Weil, in his book describing the origins of the Foreign Service, argues that the career patterns of the State Department's East European specialists had important consequences for American foreign policy in the early years of the Cold War.[45] Many of the diplomats who held high State Department positions after the Second World War began their careers in East European capitals where they lived and worked with a declining aristocracy. Since several of these diplomats had come from wealthy and conservative families they naturally had sympathy for the European upper classes, but even those Foreign Service officers from families of modest means acquired an attachment to the European nobility threatened by fascism and communism. Americans in Europe, Weil claims, did not understand the socialist forces rising in the West and their only knowledge of Russia came from contact with emigrés. As a result of this early professional experience the generation of Foreign Service officers who influenced American policy in the 1940s was inclined to automatically mistrust and generally misunderstand the Soviet Union, exaggerating the threat of international communism. The architects of containment were, according to Weil, building a policy that reflected their own prejudices as much as it did the realities of the postwar world. They constituted an elite because, regardless of their class origins, they held in common relatively uniform opinions about the world and thought themselves uniquely qualified by their experiences to dictate American foreign policy. "On one point... all diplomats, highbrow and low were united—that foreign policy should be run from the foreign office, not from the White House or Congress."[46] A bureaucratic elite, especially the elite produced by the Foreign Service, rather than being timid about exercising power, sees itself as the only group capable of exercising power and considers its particular perspective on international problems to be the essence of wisdom.

The complaint that a conservative elite had excessive influence in the formation of American foreign policy, particularly in the period after the Second World War, was echoed by a similar complaint from the other side of the political spectrum during the late 1960s and early 1970s. Presidents Johnson and Nixon sometimes described the State Department, the CIA and the Arms Control and Disarmament Agency as dangerously liberal organizations dominated by an East coast "establishment" which no longer supported American policy in Southeast Asia. Whether one sees excessive conservative or liberal influence in the foreign policy bureaucracies, the general critique of those organizations remains the same: because of the background or ideology of the individuals who hold responsible positions in the foreign affairs organizations, those organizations will not loyally serve elected officials with whom they disagree.

Where elitism in the American foreign policy bureaucracies is regarded as evidence of economic and class interest at work, no solution short of revolutionary social change could really affect the situation. Some efforts have been made to insure that the Foreign Service does not recruit too heavily from one region of the country or from a limited list of colleges and universities, and all government organizations have felt pressure to meet affirmative action goals. It will take some time before it can be determined if these new recruiting practices have a significant impact on the Foreign Service and foreign policy. According to the radical theorists of elitism these personnel policy changes will not make much difference. As long as the prevailing

American ideology supports the interests of large corporations and wealthy individuals any group of bureaucrats will consciously or unwittingly serve the purpose of the ruling class. Nor would a more democratic policy process necessarily be a solution since these foreign policy critics occasionally describe the American public as victims of a "false consciousness."

The more moderate version of elitism in the foreign policy bureaucracies does not involve class or economic interests. Instead, the problem is that organizational experiences as well as common backgrounds tend to produce bureaucrats with opinions or ideologies at variance from those of the general public or their political leaders. Presidents Franklin Roosevelt and Richard Nixon, for very different reasons, distrusted the professional foreign policy organizations they found when they came into office. Both approached this problem in the same way; they ignored their Secretary of State and Foreign Service advisers on important issues and ran foreign policy from the White House. Nixon did this more often and more completely than Roosevelt, but both wanted to avoid giving policy authority to organizations that demonstrated a bias which the president did not share. Many observers consider this presidential response to be worse than the bureaucratic problem.[47] They argue that even if the foreign policy organizations are staffed by individuals with opinions that presidents do not share, they are also staffed by individuals with indispensable expertise. The problem is to utilize the latter without being misguided by the former. No simple formula exists for the realization of this ideal combination.

Proposals designed to control organization elites are sometimes similar to the reforms addressed to the unchecked bureaucracy. Some observers suggest the creation of competing centers of expertise that will soften the problem of agency elitism by, at least, producing competing elites. Others recommend that foreign policy organizations, and particularly the State Department, remain open to lateral entry at the senior level. In addition, it is frequently proposed that career patterns in organizations be designed to give junior members a variety of assignments, some of which would include temporary duty with other departments and congressional staffs. All of this is intended to prevent the formation of an institutional leadership with distorted values, but it is hard to imagine that any or all of these measures would work. Keeping foreign policy organizations open or establishing competing agencies might mitigate the problem of bureaucratic elites, but only by aggravating other problems. Lateral entry prevents an organization from being too parochial, but makes junior members discouraged about the prospects for promotion. Broadening career patterns may be useful, but it may also involve creating new assignments and making the organization larger. Setting up competing centers of expertise throughout the government might insure that political leaders hear diverse advice, but it would surely make the government more cumbersome and more difficult to coordinate.

CONCLUSION

Throughout the postwar era the Foreign Service has been under constant and sometimes contradictory pressures to admit more people and to eliminate over-staffing; to develop expertise concerning both the issues and the nations involved in international relations and to remain sensitive to changes in American society and to the complexities of our internal decision-making process; to be more excellent and less elitist; to be less timid about policy changes and less assertive about departmental prerogatives. In a sense the list of complaints against the State Department and its personnel practices is representative of the whole problem of bureaucracy in American foreign policy. A similar list of complaints could be made after examining the social backgrounds, career patterns, or shared experiences in the military services or the CIA. The point is, that for any of these organizations a long, and not necessarily consistent, catalogue of criticisms can be found in the literature on American foreign policy.

While it is widely agreed that bureaucrats and bureaucratic organizations contribute to the failures of American performance in international relations, there seems to be no single or simple explanation of what is wrong with the foreign affairs bureaucracies or what should be done about it. The problem has been repeatedly examined during the last four decades, but as I.

M. Destler points out the "studies of foreign affairs organization have fed substantially on other studies, tending to raise the same issues and repeat (or reject) the same proposals."[48] The intractable character of bureaucratic problems is so widely accepted that for many observers the real problem is not deciding how to reform our national security organizations, but simply learning to live with them.

TWO

Bureaucratic Politics

Though the participants in Washington policymaking have a number of explanations of the bureaucratic problem in American foreign policy and a variety of contradictory reforms for its resolution, the academic world has only one widely accepted model explaining bureaucratic behavior and its effect on the foreign policymaking process. That model, as developed in the research of Graham Allison and Morton Halperin, is usually referred to as "bureaucratic politics."[1]

To the ordinary citizen the words, "bureaucratic politics," probably bring to mind a number of negative images. The French sociologist, Michel Crozier, believes that in its most familiar usage the word bureaucracy "evokes the slowness, the ponderousness, the routine, the complication of procedures, and the maladapted responses of . . . organizations to the needs which they should satisfy, and the frustrations which their members, clients, or subjects consequently endure."[2] The word "politics," for many Americans, also has a pejorative connotation. The implication behind the accusation that someone (even a politician) has "played politics" with an issue is that unnecessary delay, extraneous influence, simple-minded partisanship and selfish interests have been introduced into matters that should have been handled in a routine and impartial way. The combination of the words "bureaucratic" and "politics" suggests to the casual reader a meeting of confusion and corruption that is unlikely to produce anything worthwhile. That first impression turns out to be a somewhat exaggerated, but nevertheless accurate, summary of the studies of bureaucratic politics in American foreign policy.

MODELS OF BUREUCRATIC POLITICS IN AMERICAN FOREIGN POLICY

Like the observers of Washington policymaking, the authors of the bureaucratic politics model want to explain failures and shortcomings in American foreign policy, and they begin their analysis by describing an ideal policymaking process from which bureaucratic politics deviates. In many ways their most important observation about bureaucratic politics is not the description of what it is, but the description of what it is not. Bureaucratic politics is not rational actor policymaking.

The rational actor model, as described by Graham Allison and mentioned in most studies of bureaucratic politics, is important because it is a common academic approach to the study of foreign policymaking and because it implicitly describes the way policy should be made in an ideal situation. The rational actor model assumes that states are unified actors, that they have goals and objectives which can be clearly stated, and that all alternative policies are carefully examined before an optimum course of action is chosen.[3] In this model political scientists presume states to be rational and in pursuit of their national interests in the same way that economists presume individuals to be rational in the satisfaction of their personal desires.

Two problems emerge when one examines this model and compares it to what we know about how states and their political leaders and institutions actually behave. First, it is obvious, even to those who use rational actor analysis, that states are not unified, coherent entities. The most authoritarian dictator is never free to act with complete independence and most states make policy by a series of compromises among political leaders, institutions and interest groups. As a rule policymaking in foreign affairs is more independent than in domestic politics, but it is always subject to some restraints. Second, and of more importance, rational actor models are defective because they presume that it is possible to consider all the information and options relevant to a particular decision. In fact, this is almost never possible. Problems in foreign affairs are tremendously complex; and political leaders, even when they are supported by large staffs, do not have the time or the physical capacity to absorb all the information or calculate all the consequences that would be required for fully rational behavior.

Though the rational actor model does not describe what actually occurs, or even what could occur, it does provide the standard against which actual decisionmaking is measured. The authors who discuss bureaucratic politics apparently assume that foreign policy decisions would ideally be made by an independent political leader, with a clear set of policy goals, a full grasp of all the facts and alternatives available and the ability to calculate the particular course of action which would optimize the achievement of those policy goals. This ideal is rarely approached because bureaucratic routines and political ambitions distort the policymaking process.

In Graham Allison's work there are two models of state behavior offered as alternatives to the rational actor model, which together constitute bureaucratic politics. The first alternative, "organizational process," generally deals with the lower levels of a bureaucratic hierarchy and the second, "governmental politics," describes the interactions of senior career, appointed, and elected officials. Both suggest that rational state behavior is impossible because organizations and individuals act according to their own interests, perspectives, and habits. All of Allison's analyses of the various models of foreign policy decisionmaking are made in connection with a detailed case study of what is widely regarded as one of the foreign policy triumphs of the 1960s—the performance of the Kennedy administration during the Cuban missile crisis. Nevertheless, Allison attributes a number of errors and anomalous incidents to the consequences of organizational process and governmental politics.

When Allison refers to organizational process he is speaking of those routine responses, standard operating procedures, and petty organizational rules and interests which often interfere with effective performance of duties, particularly in extraordinary or unusual situations. Put more simply, organizations, because of their size and complexity, naturally generate what Robert Lovett testifying before the Jackson subcommittee called the "foul-up factor."[4] Allison lists the foul-ups during the Cuban missile crisis, and it makes an impressive list.

Photographic surveillance of Cuba was delayed by juris-dictional squabbles between the Air Force and the CIA; initial interpretations of intelligence data were wrong because the evidence of Soviet missile construction did not conform with expectations; orders for the removal of American missiles from Turkey were bogged down in the State Department, producing considerable embarrassment at the height of the crisis; and important details of the naval blockade were initially based on standard naval practices instead of necessary diplomatic con-siderations.[5] When organizational processes contributed to the successful handling of the missile crisis, they often did so by accident. The refusal of the Air Force to guarantee complete destruction of Soviet missiles in Cuba, which helped to eliminate the air strike alternative, was based on inadequate information about air defense in Cuba and an American military habit of preferring full scale operations to "surgical" strikes.[6] All of these examples reflect the familiar criticisms of bureaucracies as slow, parochial, inflexible, routinized and self-interested. Bureaucra-cies, even in crisis situations, allow their limited perspectives, habitual responses, and petty competitions to have important, if usually unintended, consequences. Bureaucracies bungle.

While the way organizational processes affect state behavior is something that analysts, presidents, and senior officials need to understand, it is only half of Allison's version of the bureaucratic problem. The other half involves the political relationships among senior bureaucrats, high ranking appointed officials, White House staff members, and virtually anyone whose opin-ions are sought by presidents in the course of making foreign policy decisions. These individuals possess a variety of pre-judices, interests, loyalties and ambitions. They may sincerely wish to serve the president or the national interest; they may have plans to seek elective office or appointed promotion; they may share the president's party affiliation and political philosophy or they may have been solicited to provide balance and expertise. Generally, they have in common a need to court favor with the chief executive, but their relationships with him are always ambiguous, leaving open the question of who serves whom. The competition among those with presidential access and influence to control policy is a process which both Allison and Morton Halperin describe as a game, the final outcome of which significantly depends upon the gamesmanship of the players rather than their substantive positions on the issues. In the case of the Cuban missile crisis, the political skills and special confidence of the president possessed by Robert Kennedy, Robert McNamara and Theodore Sorensen contributed to the "excom" blockade decision, despite serious arguments and influential proponents for more moderate and more forceful courses of action.[7]

The governmental politics model may also be accurately called a bureaucratic politics model, because the demarcation between professional and political administrators in the American federal government is blurred and because almost everyone in Washington represents some organization in some degree. Allison, in an article with Halperin, agrees that his organizational process and governmental politics models can be collapsed into a single analytical framework.[8] Presidential appointments cover a wide range of offices and the group of people influencing presidential action include civil servants, party loyalists, issue experts, military officers, technocrats and business leaders. Some appointees hold office under different parties and many under different presidents, some are appointed after a government career and many have had extensive experience in civil, foreign or military service. As a rule presidents are surrounded by bureaucrats and by appointed officials whose loyalties are often divided between the politician who appointed them and the organization they lead and represent. Governmental politics is primarily the competition of these people for presidential recognition and policy influence. Allison argues that in this competition organizational affiliation is a good predictor of the position that an individual will take, and that the reasons put forward in support of a particular policy are often rationalizations for organizational interests. When the competition is especially intense players do more than rationalize. The game includes leaks of classified or damaging information, intentionally biased reporting, false recommendations made to make the preferred recommendation look better, and a whole catalogue of bureaucratic maneuvers to delay or alter decisions. This is not the bureaucracy that bungles policy, this is the bureaucracy that makes and sometimes sabotages policy. The fact that things worked out well in the Cuban missile crisis is no guarantee that favorable outcomes will be normal. In fact, the isolation, informality, and level of substantive debate in the "excom" were exceptional and do not reflect most governmental politics.

Morton Halperin's *Bureaucratic Politics and Foreign Policy* is, in many ways, a manual for the playing of the governmental politics game.[9] Halperin recognizes the first bureaucratic problem—the consequences of routine procedures, limited perspectives, and petty organization rivalries—but his principal concern is with the actions of high level agency personnel and their control over policy outcomes. He argues that the bargaining of competing centers of bureaucratic power often produces contradictory and confusing national security decisions. In particular he explains how the Johnson administradtion commitment to build a "light" ABM system, announced by McNamara in a speech condemning the principle of strategic missile defense, was an illogical compromise among conflicting bureaucratic politicians. Many of those who use Allison's and Halperin's models in studies of military or foreign policy decisions find that the waste, inefficiency or ineffectiveness of American actions can be traced to the bureaucratic character of decisionmaking in American government.

The observation that the government of the United States is not a rational actor does not preclude extremely rational action on the part of bureaucratic gamesmen. Halperin tells us that the skillful and determined bureaucrat will leak *favorable* information about competitors for presidential influence in order to discredit them as publicity seekers.[10] In addition he will be prepared to pass information, some of which may be classified, to Congress, interest groups, the press and perhaps to foreign governments. He may even be willing to resign, if resignation can be expected to advance his cause. He will strategically plan committee meetings and social engagements in order to maximize exposure to influential people, and he will form tacit or formal alliances with members of an opposition party, rival bureaucratic agencies, the devil or Jack Anderson, if need be.

Viewed close up, the vantage point of the bureaucratic politics approach, everything about policymaking appears to be organizational and personal interest. The only individual likely to be fully concerned about the good of the nation is the president, but he is at the mercy of conflicting and manipulative advisers in charge of bureaucracies that both bungle and sabotage presidential instructions. It is difficult to see how any policy can be made from such materials.

Given this constant and sometimes desperate competition for policy influence, it is hard for the bureaucratic politics model to account for those occasions when complicated or controversial policies are actually carried out. Halperin reassures us that there are some limits to bureaucratic politics.[11] The first is provided by the president. The fact that there is a single individual ultimately responsible for American foreign policy and clearly more powerful than any other individual, means that most players in a particular policy game must protect their influence with the president in order to participate in future contests. Bureaucratic politics is more intense before a president makes a decision or indicates his preference, and less intense if a president makes it clear that his decision or preference is final and important.

The other factor which limits the range and intensity of bureaucratic political competition is the existence of a set of "shared assumptions" or images that are held by virtually all government officials. Policymaking rarely involves the reevaluation of these assumptions. Some, like the need for an adequate national defense, are general and perennial; others, like the need to prevent communist expansion in Southeast Asia, are controversial and influential for a particular period of time. In books about bureaucratic politics very little attention is given to the origins of these assumptions or to the processes by which they change. As described by Halperin, these "shared assumptions" reflect the basic ideas and events that shape a particular generation and, to some degree, must be produced by the results of old bureaucratic battles. Like the overall behavior of nations, these assumptions are not fully rational. Though they do help to hold competing bureaucratic organizations together, the real bureaucratic problem may be the apparent inability of organizations and individuals to evaluate and escape the limitations of unrealistic or outdated images and assumptions about the world.

BUREAUCRATIC POLITICS AND REFORM

Though the models of bureaucratic politics are usually presented as analytical tools for explaining foreign policy decisions, they also contain descriptions of the bureaucratic problems in the making of foreign policy and suggest strategies for minimizing those problems. In this context the distinction between Allison's two models is important, even if it is a distinction difficult to draw in practice. At its core the difference between organizational processes and governmental politics is a matter of intentions. In the organizational process model, bureaucrats inadvertently reduce the effectiveness of American foreign policy by seeing problems from a narrow point of view, by acting out of habit, and by failing to understand the consequences of their procedures. In the governmental politics model members of organizations, and usually the senior members, compete for control of decisions, and although that competition is constrained, it often involves deliberate efforts to manipulate information, to resist instructions, and even to violate laws in pursuit of important policy outcomes. In reality it is often difficult to tell the difference between a long delay in implementation due to procedural routines and one due to calculated disloyalty. It is also hard to decide whether a demand for a larger military budget is primarily based on organizational interests or serious deficiencies in the nation's defense. Perceptions and deceptions get very confused in the literature on bureaucratic politics. The difference between unintentional and intentional bureaucratic problems is, however, extremely important in the reorganization and reform of government organizations.

The problems of organizational process can never be completely eliminated, especially in foreign affairs where the organizations involved are necessarily large and where rapidly changing events are likely to make some procedures outdated and inappropriate. But these problems could be reduced by coordination of government agencies and monitoring of important operational matters by a small central staff responsive to high level political officials. Such a staff would, at least, be able to catch the worst operational process errors. This was, in fact, the way that Kennedy and his senior advisers handled the Cuban missile crisis and the way a number of presidents have tried to manage their foreign policies. The problem with this solution is that it could produce problems in terms of government politics. A powerful centralized staff easily becomes another new bureaucracy capable of putting its own pressures on a president.

The central problem in all models of bureaucratic politics is that the president, or any individual, lacks the time, ability, and information to unravel the complex interests, motives, and rationalizations that affect a single policy decision, much less the myriad of decisions that must be made at any given time. Presidents must delegate responsibility and if there is intense governmental politics among the advisers to a president, decentralization, rather than centralization, is probably advisable. A president who wanted to maintain flexibility and personal control over his staff and administration would logically multiply the number of organizations and experts that provide him with information and options. This would make it likely that policy arguments that were patent rationalizations would be recognized as such, and it would, by increasing policy competition, increase the dependence of each individual and organization on presidential attention. Naturally, decentralizing advice and expertise also creates organizational process problems and by no means guarantees that presidents will make correct choices.

The tension between solving organizational process problems through centralization and solving governmental political problems through decentralization has been at the heart of debates about how the government should be organized for the conduct of foreign affairs for the last forty years. But the theorists of bureaucratic politics do not suggest that either centralization or decentralization would constitute a solution to the bureaucratic problem in American foreign policy. In fact, no real solution is possible. The authors of the studies of bureaucratic politics describe a policymaking system that will always be influenced by organizational and personal interests and their principal concern is that analysts, political leaders, and citizens understand these bureaucratic realities. Understanding bureaucratic politics might make presidents more effective players in the policymaking game. It might make academics and citizens more sympathetic toward policymakers who must act in an extraordinarily complex system. And it might make it possible for reformers to institute limited changes in the balance of bureaucratic power in Washington which might marginally improve the policymaking process.

This is what Allison, Destler, and others end up proposing.[12]

Believing that bureaucratic politics is an important factor in the making of foreign policy, and recognizing that organizational distortions of policymaking can never be eliminated, they suggest reforms which have the limited purpose of altering the distribution of power among existing foreign policy bureaucracies. All organizations will have certain perspectives, biases and interests, but some perspectives, biases and interests are more likely than others to produce good policy. Thus, they favor strengthening the position of the Secretary of State and the State Department and weakening the position of the national security adviser and the NSC, because they believe that the interests and biases of the permanent department most familiar with world affairs are more likely to result in good policy advice than those of a White House staff.[13] Even if this were true, and the changes recommended by students of bureaucratic politics were made, it would not eliminate the struggle between the national security adviser and the Secretary of State, or between the Secretary of State and the Secretary of Defense, or among all the individuals and organizations that have a part to play in the making of foreign policy. It would only increase the probability that a particular player in the policymaking game would win more often.

For those who accept the validity of the models of bureaucratic politics, there is no reform which can remove organizational processes and perspectives or individual biases and interests from American foreign policy. Bureaucratic politics is a reality which must be accepted by presidents, by policymakers, by citizens, and by reformers. No matter what is done about the bureaucratic problem in American foreign policy there will always be occasions when bureaucracies bungle and bureaucrats sabotage the policies of our highest elected representatives.

CONCLUSION

The models of bureaucratic politics focus attention on how options and information flow to the top of organizations and suggest that rational decisionmaking is impossible because bureaucracies and bureaucrats introduce their own perspectives, interests, routines, and ambitions into the decisionmaking process. The central decisionmaker, in the case of American foreign policy, the president, is either the unwitting victim of bureaucratic politics or just another player in the policymaking game. He may be a more powerful player than others, and he may be the only player with an institutional perspective that encourages a broad view of issues and a respect for public opinion, but in the end he cannot escape the need for organizations and advisers and the inevitable bureaucratic problems that accompany them. Political leaders will always find that they are poorly served by the organizations and advisers ostensibly there to assist them. No reform can prevent this from happening.

But an even more serious problem is implicit in the models of bureaucratic politics. Political leaders are, in these models, almost indistinguishable from bureaucrats. Both politicians and bureaucrats are decisionmakers; both have partial, never complete, access to relevant information; both have preferences and assumptions about the world and about policy that are partly personal and partly institutional; and both have an impact, to a greater or lesser degree, on the formal and informal bargaining processes which produce policy. There is a legal hierarchy among those responsible for foreign affairs but discipline is loose, loyalties are diverse, and in relationships between principals and advisers it is never clear who controls whom. The major determinants of policy outcomes are organizational interests, personal ambitions, and shared assumptions. And political leaders have relatively little power over any of these.

If all of this is true, the most critical bureaucratic problem in American foreign policy may not be that leaders are ill served by bureaucrats; it may be that our political leaders are themselves bureaucrats.

THREE

Statesmanship And Bureaucracy

Since the earliest recognition of the growing importance of bureaucratization in western civilization, thoughtful observers have argued that the critical problem in a bureaucratic age will not be how to control large organizations, but whether or not there will be anyone willing and able to do so. Max Weber, whose description of ideal bureaucracy gives some the impression that he was an advocate of bureaucratization, was, in fact, just the opposite. In his public career as a journalist, a speaker, and an opinion leader, he regularly protested the influence of bureaucracies in the German economy and government, and particularly the influence of bureaucrats in the conduct of German foreign policy. Weber's popular writings and private conversations were filled with apprehension that a bureaucratized world, especially one in which organizations were rational and efficient, would be a world without creativity, without purpose, without soul.

> It is horrible to think that the world could one day be filled with nothing but those little cogs, little men clinging to little jobs and striving towards bigger ones—a state of affairs which is to be seen once more, as in the Egyptian records, playing an ever increasing part in the spirit of our present administrative system, and especially of its offspring, the students. This passion for bureaucracy ... is enough to drive one to despair. It is as if in politics ... we were deliberately to become men who need "order" and nothing but order, who become nervous and cowardly if for one moment

this order wavers, and helpless if they are torn away
from their total incorporation in it. That the world
should know no men but these—it is in such an
evolution that we are already caught up, and the great
question is therefore not how we can promote and
hasten it, but what can we oppose to this machinery in
order to keep a portion of mankind free from this
parcelling out of the soul, from this supreme mastery
of the bureaucratic way of life.[1]

In his academic career Weber devoted much of his energy
and intellect to an examination of the causes and consequences
of bureaucratization. In both his popular and scholarly writing
he made distinctions between politics and administration,
between statesmen and bureaucrats, and between democratic
and bureaucratic foreign policies. Many of these same distinctions were also made by Henry Kissinger in his academic
research and writing. Reviewing what Weber and Kissinger have
to say about bureaucracy will provide us with a new account of
the bureaucratic problem in American foreign policy. This new
version of the problem has little to do with how organizations are
structured, staffed, or coordinated, or the extent to which they are
subject to bureaucratic politics. Instead, it draws attention to the
relationship between leaders and bureaucrats and asks whether a
bureaucratic age can produce the qualities essential for effective
leadership.

WEBER ON POLITICIANS AND BUREAUCRATS

At the end of the First World War Weber wrote a series of articles
analyzing the causes of the war and the prospects for creating a
viable German government. The articles, entitled "Parliament
and Government in a Reconstructed Germany," explore the
relationship between bureaucracies and legislative bodies, and
between civil servants and politicians. Weber's arguments in
these essays for a strengthened parliament and for universal
suffrage were unconventional and were not incorporated in the
Weimar Constitution, but they do provide useful insights into his

understanding of the nature of the bureaucratic problem and its consequences for foreign affairs.

Politics, Weber observes early in the articles, can be defined as conflict.[2] It involves the struggle over fundamental principles, the recruitment of allies and popular support, the competition for power, and the assumption of responsibility associated with the use of power.[3] Civil servants, as opposed to politicians, are accustomed to a minimum of struggle. They acquire a sense of duty, rather than a sense of responsibility. They engage in calculation rather than principled debate; they act out of obedience rather than conviction. Weber argues that the central problem for Germany in the pre-war decades was that "men with a bureaucratic mentality" were put "into positions of political leadership" for which they were by temperament and training ill-equipped.[4]The origin of Germany's problems in the 20th century can be traced to Bismarck and his refusal to share political power. Bismarck left Germany "without any political sophistication" and with a parliament that was "nothing but the unwillingly tolerated rubber stamp of a ruling bureaucracy."[5] National political parties, which before Bismarck's rule were principled voluntary organizations, rapidly deteriorated into aggregates of special interest representatives. Having eliminated opposition from the legislature and the political parties, Bismarck was able to exercise unchallenged rule, but in the process he destroyed the chances that he would be followed by an equally powerful or competent successor.[6]

In a sense the "Bismarck legacy" was only the immediate cause of Germany's problem in the years before the First World War; the underlying cause, according to Weber, was the bureaucratization of all Western societies that accompanied the modernization of their economies and the democratization of their politics. Bureaucratic organizations in factories, armies, political parties and public agencies were acquiring extensive power in every European country and in America. "The present world war means the world-wide triumph of this form of life, which was advancing at any rate."[7] Weber raises three questions about this general trend. The first is whether individual freedom can survive bureaucratization; and he suggests that without the European liberal tradition of the "Rights of Man" it cannot. Even with that tradition the prospects for genuine liberty are diminishing in the modern world. The second question is whether any power centers exist in Western societies that could challenge and check the growing dominance of the state bureaucracies. Weber mentions two such power centers—private corporations and a powerful legislature. Throughout "Parliament and Government in a Reconstructed Germany" Weber argues for a strong Reichstag; elsewhere he defends capitalism by pointing out that corporate bureaucracies might be needed to counterbalance state agencies.[8]

The third and most important question deals with the "inherent limitations of bureaucracy proper."[9] The fundamental limitation of bureaucratic organization is its inability to produce its own leadership. "The 'directing-mind,' the 'moving spirit'— that of the entrepreneur here and of the politician there—differs in substance from the civil-service mentality of the official . . . .If a man in a leading position is an 'official' in the spirit of his performance, no matter how qualified—a man, that is, who works dutifully and honorably according to rules and instruction—then he is as useless at the helm of a private enterprise as of a government."[10] This does not mean that bureaucrats do dull, unimportant, routine work and that entrepreneurs and politicians perform the interesting and intellectually demanding tasks in the world. Nor does it mean that men of genius are needed to found corporations and rule nations. Weber does not suggest that there is a simple dichotomy between politics and administration as early theorists of public administration tended to do. In fact, the problem Weber saw in the conduct of German affairs was the inevitable blurring of politics and administration and the unfortunate fact that men trained for one kind of activity ended up performing the other. Weber's point is that there is a difference between the kinds of responsibility which officials and leaders are willing and accustomed to assume. In a conflict between duty and conscience, the official is expected to choose duty. "A political leader acting this way would deserve contempt."[11] Germany's problem before the First World War and especially in the conduct of foreign affairs, Weber argues, was the lack of "*direction* of the state by a *politician*—not by a political genius, to be expected only once every few centuries, not even by a great political talent, but simply by a politician."[12]

Weber goes on to show how a weak German parliament, unable to recruit or promote able members, unwilling actively to investigate and challenge the bureaucracy, left vital decisions to the monarch and his bureaucratic advisers. Kaiser Wilhelm II, in Weber's opinion, made a series of disastrous mistakes from the Kruger telegram to the *Daily Telegraph* interview which strengthened the coalition against Germany. These actions by the Kaiser often involved the publication of private statements by "sedulous court officials or news services, either with the toleration or even with the participation of the government."[13] Weber does not criticize the Kaiser directly for these incidents, and instead attacks the monarch's advisers who were not "experienced in weighing the effects of public statements."[14] They did not know that the Kaiser's words would inhibit secret diplomacy and inflame foreign populations. What made matters worse was that even when these advisers suspected that the Kaiser was in error, they still carried out his wishes:

> Here the abyss that separates the two can be seen most clearly. The civil servant must sacrifice his convictions to the demands of obedience; the politician must publicly reject the responsibility for political actions that run counter to his convictions and must sacrifice his office to them. But in Germany this has never happened. . . . It is reliably known that almost all of the men who were in charge of our policies in that disastrous decade have time and again privately repudiated grave declarations for which they accepted formal responsibility. If one asked with amazement why a statesman remained in office if he was powerless to prevent the publication of a questionable statement, the usual answer was that 'somebody else would have been found' to authorize it.[15]

Weber believes it was very significant that none of the pre-war foreign policy disasters produced important resignations; instead the prestige of the monarch and the nation was constantly staked on ill-advised positions until military force was needed to repair diplomatic errors.

Weber proposes that the German constitution be rewritten

giving extensive power to the Reichstag and ensuring that ministers are selected from the legislature rather than the civil service. He favors universal suffrage and defends it against those who fear demagoguery. Germany already suffers, Weber claims, from demagogic activities by the monarch and his ministers who carry out their intrigues in the press and in public meetings. Furthermore, the demagogue is not necessarily worse than the bureaucrat. "The decisive point is that for the tasks of national leadership only such men are prepared who have been selected in the course of the political struggle. . . . It simply happens to be a fact that such preparation is, on the average, accomplished better by the much-maligned 'craft of demagoguery' than by the clerk's office."[16] Weber does not favor open diplomacy or public legislative debates of foreign affairs. "Everywhere, and particularly in a democracy, the big decisions in foreign policy are made by a small number of persons."[17] Nor does Weber argue for democracy because he trusts the opinions or the wisdom of the masses.[18] His defense of democratic reforms in suffrage and in the power of the legislature are based almost exclusively on his argument that Germany needs a constitutional system which will produce responsible political leadership and on his contention that "politicians must be the countervailing force against bureaucratic domination."[19]

KISSINGER ON BUREAUCRATS AND STATESMEN

For Weber the danger in a highly bureaucratized society is not that bureaucracies will be inefficient or irrational in the accomplishment of organization goals, or that they will necessarily serve their political leaders disloyally. The more critical problem is that such a society will find it difficult to produce leaders capable of understanding, articulating, or committing themselves to important goals, and that, in the absence of such leadership, drift and disorder will prevail regardless of the performance or proficiency of particular bureaucracies.

Almost identical arguments can be found in the academic works of Henry Kissinger. In his studies of 19th century statesmanship and in his analysis of American foreign policy, Kissinger emphasized the need for creativity, innovation, and grand designs in foreign affairs increasingly dominated by domestic bureaucratic structures. Kissinger both echoes and refines the distinctions found in Weber's essays.

Almost all of Kissinger's scholarly work contains some observations about the relationship between bureaucrats and statesmen. Even in his first book, a study of European relations in the second decade of the 19th century, Kissinger outlined the essential difference between the demands of domestic politics and the nature of international relations. The statesman, Kissinger observes at the end of *A World Restored,* must be able to cultivate domestic support for his diplomacy by justifying his policy to other government officials and by harmonizing it with the historical experience of his nation. The first of these two tasks is always difficult and frequently occupied the time and energies of Metternich and Castlereagh. The problem, as Kissinger explains it, is an inherent tension between policy and bureaucracy. The two are diametrically opposed.

> The essence of policy is its contingency; its success depends on the correctness of an estimate which is in part conjectural. The essence of bureaucacy is its quest for safety; its success is calculability. Profound policy thrives on perpetual creation, on a constant redefinition of goals. Good administration thrives on routine, the definition of relationships which can survive mediocrity. Policy involves an adjustment of risks; administration an avoidance of deviation. Policy justifies itself by the relationship of its measures and its sense of proportion; administration by the rationality of each action in terms of a given goal. The attempt to conduct policy bureaucratically leads to a quest for calculability which tends to become a prisoner of events. The effort to administer politically leads to total irresponsibility, because bureaucracies are designed to execute, not to conceive.... The attempt to define social goals bureaucratically will, therefore, always lead to the distortion inherent in applying a rationality of means to the development of ends.[20]

In all of his books Kissinger differentiates between foreign policy and domestic administration. The former requires creativity, innovation, risk, a profound understanding of national experience and values, and a willingness to alter those values in the face of changes in the international environment. The latter requires organization, routine, certainty, specialized technical training, and the use of instrumental rationality to maximize established values. Both Metternich and Castlereagh were statesmen who, though often distracted by the demands of dealing with domestic bureaucracies, were temporarily successful in managing these challenges to their foreign policy.[21]

While Kissinger saw statesmanship triumphing over bureaucracy in the years following the Napoleonic wars, he saw the opposite in the making of American foreign policy after the Second World War. Both of the books he wrote in the 1950s analyzing the central strategic and diplomatic problems facing the United States end with critical evaluations of the quality of American leadership. At the conclusion of *Nuclear Weapons and Foreign Policy* Kissinger makes a distinction between "inspiration" and "organization" which is similar to the comment about "policy" and "bureaucracy" found in *A World Restored.*

> Organization expresses the importance of continuity; the routine by which it operates represents a recognition that a society must be able to assimilate and utilize mediocrity. Inspiration, on the other hand, is the mechanism of growth; it is the ability to transcend a framework which has come to be taken for granted.[22]

Obviously a balance is needed between organization and inspiration, but in modern societies, and particularly in the United States, this balance is increasingly hard to achieve. Contemporary organizations are so large and complex that their leaders become preoccupied with internal administrative problems and no longer have the time or ability to reflect on the purposes for which organizations were originally created. The training of organizational managers reinforces this disregard for purpose. "The skill required in attaining eminence within a large administrative mechanism is essentially manipulative. . . . But the qualities required for leadership are primarily creative. ... The pattern of thinking developed in the rise to eminence may, therefore, inhibit effectiveness once eminence has been reached."[23] The situation in America is made still worse by our history of isolation and our empiricist faith in expertise. American leadership groups recruited from among business and legal professionals are "better prepared to deal with technical than with conceptual problems, with economic than with political issues."[24]

The critique of American political leadership continues in *The Necessity for Choice* where Kissinger observes that the typical cabinet or sub-cabinet officer in America lacks "the combination of political acumen, conceptual skill, persuasive power, and substantive knowledge required for the highest positions of government."[25] Intellectuals who might be able to redress some of the deficiencies in America's leadership group rarely do so because they are either corrupted by the process of consultation and tell leaders what they want to hear, or are insensitive to the needs of policymakers and give them advice they cannot use.

All these observations are strikingly similar to Weber's analysis of Germany at the end of the First World War. Men occupying positions of power and responsibility have received their training in organizations where problems are solved by obedience to rules and technical research, and without the development of individual responsibility. They lack the ability or inclination to examine, challenge, and redefine the basic goals and purposes of their action. Politicians, at least in matters of foreign policy, are uninformed and weak. Intellectuals are disinterested or ineffectual. Unlike Weber, however, Kissinger does not propose to increase the power of the legislature to counterbalance bureaucratic influence. Nor does Kissinger fully explain the kinds of experience which would be likely to produce a successful political leader. He offers no solution to the problem of bureaucracy, except perhaps the fortuitous appearance of a creative individual able and willing to dominate the policy-making process.

Kissinger's most elaborate statement about the effect of bureaucracy on international relations is contained in his essay, "Domestic Structure and Foreign Policy."[26] In it, Kissinger repeats his analysis of the character and deficiencies of Ameri-

can leadership and compares America's rulers to their communist and third world counterparts. In all three cases leadership
style is a product of domestic structure and national experience,
and the primary characteristic of both Western and communist
domestic politics is the existence of bureaucracy.

Kissinger admits the need for bureaucratic administration,
especially in modern complex societies. However, "increased
control over the domestic environment is purchased at the price
of loss of flexibility in international affairs."[27] This loss of flexibility occurs for a number of reasons. Bureaucracy absorbs the
time and energy of its leadership, making reflection about the
substance of decisions more difficult. Leaders increasingly
preoccupied with administrative problems become the prisoners
of their advisers and their advisers, in turn, become the prisoners
of events. Bureaucrats seek certainty even where it does not
exist.

> The quest for 'objectivity'—while desirable theoreti-
> cally—involves the danger that means and ends are
> confused, that an average standard of performance is
> exalted as the only valid one. Attention tends to be
> diverted from the act of choice—which is the ultimate
> test of statesmanship—to the accumulation of facts.
> Decisions can be avoided until a crisis brooks no
> further delay, until the events themselves have re-
> moved the element of ambiguity. But at that point the
> scope for constructive action is at a minimum.
> Certainty is purchased at the cost of creativity.[28]

Under these circumstances foreign policy is characterized by a
combination of rigidity and arbitrariness. Once a decision is
made by a complex organization it may be extremely difficult to
change. When change occurs, it is often achieved by extra-
bureaucratic means. "It is a paradoxical aspect of modern
bureaucracies that their quest for objectivity and calculability
often leads to impasses which can be overcome only by
essentially arbitrary decisions."[29] The normal difficulties in
coordinating and changing policies are so great that eventually
dramatic and unauthorized action becomes necessary if any
progress is to be made.

The existence of a bureaucratic domestic structure reduces the scope and effectiveness of diplomacy, between allies and adversaries. Consultation is made more difficult "when the internal process of decisionmaking already has some of the characteristics of compacts between quasi-sovereign entities."[30] The relations of enemies already made rigid by conflicting ideologies become even more stilted when there are large bureaucracies on one or both sides. In the absence of effective diplomacy, crisis management becomes the prevalent mode of resolving disputes and the stability of the international system is weakened by the frequent shifts from rigid adherence to past policy to sudden *ad hoc* re-evaluation.

The extent of bureaucratization constitutes only one factor, though probably the most important one, in Kissinger's analysis of the relationship between domestic politics and international relations. The experience of leaders during their rise to eminence and the values of their societies combine with the domestic structure to produce distinctive leadership styles. In the United States Kissinger describes the leadership style as "bureaucratic-pragmatic." Pragmatism as a philosophy reinforced by American history and by the training of lawyers and businessmen compounds the defects of a bureaucratic administration of foreign affairs. Americans convinced that all problems can be solved in time, through research, and by compromise, are too prone to delay, to depend on expertise, and to seek consensus. They are unlikely to plan for the long range, to appreciate the nuances of a problem, or to study and understand history.

In the communist countries where the leadership is ideological the tenets of Marx and Lenin and the struggle for personal power also reinforce the defects of bureaucracy. "The essence of Marxism-Leninism—and the reason that normal diplomacy with communist states is so difficult—is the view that 'objective' factors such as the social structure, the economic process, and, above all, the class struggle are more important than the personal convictions of statesmen."[31] Like their Western counterparts communist leaders believe in the existence of "objective" solutions to problems and have confidence in their eventual success. Even more than Western leaders, the rulers of communist countries are accustomed to the constant bureaucratic struggle for power which is particularly intense and vicious in a system without any provision for legitimate succession.

Communist leaders tend to be suspicious, opportunist, and doctrinaire. Their ideology and their personal experiences make it hard for them to understand Western pragmatism or to control the rigidities of their own bureaucratic system. Despite the similarities between the bureaucratized institutions in the East and West, Kissinger does not accept any of the theories of convergence.[32] The existence of parallel problems in the domestic structure of all developed countries does not necessarily mean that an evolutionary process is bringing them closer together. In fact, just the opposite may be occurring. Since bureaucratization inhibits effective diplomacy, the likelihood is that a productive superpower dialogue will become progressively harder to achieve and maintain.

Kissinger describes a third style of leadership found predominantly in third world countries that are largely unaffected by the problems of bureaucratic administration. The "charismatic-revolutionary" leader holds power because of his personal ambition and ability to inspire others. The problem in Western dealings with the third world is that our bureaucrats often have no counterparts in these countries and our pragmatism leads us to assume that their primary interest is rapid economic development. In fact, the charismatic revolutionary may prefer to ignore economic problems which can only be solved slowly, and seek immediate recognition by dramatic action in the international arena. It is interesting to note that Kissinger regards leadership in the absence of bureaucratic institutions to be a manifestation of personal creativity and vision. In fundamental agreement with Weber, Kissinger declares, "Ours is the age of the expert, or the charismatic leader."[33]

"Domestic Structure and Foreign Policy" ends with some of Kissinger's broadest observations about the character of the contemporary international order. The dangers we face, according to Kissinger, emerge from the differences between the expert and the charismatic, between the politician and the revolutionary, and between the statesman and the prophet.[34] The history of international relations can be divided into periods in which the dominant mode of behavior was either political or prophetic. The period between the Congress of Vienna and World War I, which first attracted Kissinger's scholarly energies, was a political era. It was preceded and followed by the upheavals of the French Revolution and the world wars of the 20th century.

> Both modes have produced considerable accomplish-
> ments, though the prophetic style is likely to involve
> the greater dislocations and more suffering. Each has
> its nemesis. The nemesis of the statesman is that
> equilibrium, though it may be the condition of
> stability, does not supply its own motivation; that of
> the prophet is the impossibility of sustaining a mood
> of exaltation without the risk of submerging man in
> the vastness of a vision and reducing him to a mere
> figure to be manipulated.[35]

In our own time the statesmen of the West must deal with the revolutionaries of the third world and the ideologues of the communist world, a generation removed from their own revolution. Communication and diplomacy among these groups is inhibited by the dominance of bureaucratic institutions in the developed countries, by the differences in leadership style, and, most deeply, by differences in philosophic perspective. Westerners are products of an intellectual history which is based on a scientific understanding of the external world. This empiricist perspective has created tremendous technological progress, but has made it difficult for us to appreciate those areas of the world which continue to attach less importance to the material world than to religious beliefs or national history.

The bureaucratic problem in American foreign policy is part of this larger philosophic problem. The search for objective, scientific, and certain answers, which inevitably requires large organizations and trained experts, is a search which discounts the need for political leaders and tends to produce the world which Weber feared—a world with many little cogs and no great souls.

THE SOURCES OF STATESMANSHIP

The models of bureaucratic politics suggest that ineffective policy is the result of the routines and interests at the lower levels of organizations and the perspectives and ambitions at the middle and upper levels. The bureaucratic problem unavoidably emerges from our dependence on organizations that are bound to produce faulty information, biased recommendations, disagreements about budgets and missions, and inefficient implementation of unpopular decisions. Rational foreign policy is impossible to attain because political leaders must bargain and negotiate with their ostensible subordinates in a bureaucratic policymaking environment. While not denying the existence of organizational routines and interests, Max Weber and Henry Kissinger offer a different perspective on the bureaucratic problem. They argue that inefficiencies emerging from the bottom of organizations are less important than the lack of direction at the top. That lack of direction is related to the bureaucratic character of modern societies, not simply because bureaucracies restrain political leaders, but because they also make it unlikely that a society will produce them. In the absence of effective leadership foreign policy becomes controlled by individuals and organizations usually reluctant to exercise responsibility, apt to seek certainty and objectivity in inherently ambiguous situations, and lacking the experience and creativity needed to understand and transform the fundamental goals of a nation. The bureaucratic problem is not in the failure of organizations to accomplish given objectives rationally, but in their reluctance and inability to develop and articulate those objectives in a changing world.

Simply pointing out the lack of political leadership or statesmanship in a society or in the conduct of foreign policy is an insufficient evaluation of the bureaucratic problem. It raises at least as many questions as it answers. If organizational experience does not equip an individual for high office, what kind of experience does? If bureaucracies cannot develop national goals or values, what kinds of institutions can? If bureaucratic organizations bargain among themselves in the absence of effective leadership, how do they respond to its presence? These questions require a careful definition of what is meant by leadership and statesmanship and an explanation of where and how these qualities might be produced.

The essence of leadership in Weber's sociology of authority is the possession of personal qualities which inspire others to follow the example and instruction of the leader. Leadership is charisma, and although a bureaucratic age may be less likely to produce charismatic individuals than other historical periods, the possibility always exists that a dynamic personality will emerge and be able to dominate an organization or a society. That domination will rarely outlive the charismatic individual who exercises it, though the actions and beliefs of the leader are likely to be adopted by a succeeding bureaucratic administration. Weber's phrase describing this situation, the "routinization of charisma," suggests that extraordinary personal characteristics will allow an occasional individual to exercise broad-ranging authority, but that dramatic leaders are likely to be succeeded by less imaginative and less powerful followers.[36]Bureaucratic control of modern societies will be the norm and charismatic influences will produce infrequent periods of rapid change.

In Weber's descriptions of, and prescriptions for, German politics a more moderate definition of leadership can be found, a definition which implies that the origin of leadership is more than merely the accident of personality. The leader is an individual trained in the struggles of politics, who has participated in public conflicts, and who has been forced to make decisions and take full responsibility for their consequences. Participation in bureaucratic politics would not produce leadership qualities because the struggles are often petty, usually hidden from the public, and do not involve the assumption of responsibility for recommendations and decisions. A leader in Weber's description of German politics, is simply an experienced democratic politician, who has gained prominence within a parliament and a political party. This type of leader can be produced with some frequency by a constitution providing for a powerful and democratic legislature. Such a legislature can counter bureaucratic power if it has full investigative powers and is the institution from which ministers are selected.[37]

This legislative definition of leadership shares one defect with the broader category of charismatic authority. For both the charismatic personality and the parliamentarian-politician, Weberian leadership is divorced from the substance of political decisions or actions. Leadership comes from an attractive personality or experience in public debates, not necessarily from any connection between the leader and the positions he has taken. In the essay, "Politics as a Vocation," Weber draws an important distinction between righteously pursuing a course of action without regard for the consequences—the ethics of ultimate ends—and carefully considering the effects of political decisions—the ethics of responsibility.[38]In the final analysis Weber wants a mixture of the two, describing the "three preeminent qualities" decisive for a politician as "passion, a feeling of responsibility, and a sense of proportion."[39] Passion is primary, and it is the quality least likely to survive bureaucratization. Passion in this sense means an attachment to a cause, but causes often have no rational justification.[40] Weber criticized German politics in the period before the First World War because bureaucratic advisers to the monarch failed to understand or take responsibility for foreign policy disasters. A similar criticism could not be made for Germany in the period prior to the Second World War when the bureaucracies were dominated by a powerful political leader and when the decisions leading up to the war were clearly intended to have that effect. Weber would, no doubt, have found Nazism to be an extreme and dangerous example of the "ethics of ultimate ends" but his definitions of leadership offer no other basis for criticism of its policies and actions. The problem for the Weberian account of leadership is that the purposes for which the charismatic personality or the parliamentarian-politician exercise power are not part of that account. If the leader is preferable to the bureaucrat it is only for the passion and potential for change which he brings to politics, not for his wisdom or his superior understanding.

When we turn to Kissinger and ask the same set of questions about the origin and nature of political leadership we find a more complicated account in which the statesman is an historical figure shaped and constrained by the traditions and values of his society, but called upon to reconcile past national experience with an often dangerous international order and his own vision of the future. The relationship of the political leader to history is crucial for Kissinger. Statesmen may be revolutionary or conservative, but in either case they are measured by the extent to which they understand and have a personal impact on historical events. The task of the statesman is to preserve a realm of human freedom amidst the inevitable and unpredictable elements in human affairs. "There is a margin between necessity and accident, in which the statesman by perseverance and intuition must choose and thereby shape the destiny of his people."[41] That destiny may involve radical domestic or international upheaval as it did for Napoleon and Bismarck, or preservation of a declining order as it did for Metternich, but all statesmen, revolutionary and conservative, must be individuals able to impose their will on the course of great events.

Much of Kissinger's critique of bureaucracy involves the tendency of organizations, and individuals trained in organizations, to avoid risks, await results, and base decisions on objective and quantifiable factors. The political leader must avoid the temptation, especially prevalent in a bureaucratic society, to delay action, accumulate more information, and seek ideal solutions. Leadership requires above all else, decisiveness—the willingness to act when facts are ambiguous and when opportunities to affect events are great. "A society learns only from experience; it knows only when it is too late to act. But a statesman must act as if his inspirations were already experience, as if his aspiration were 'truth.' He must bridge the gap between a society's experience and his vision, between its tradition and its future."[42]

If the statesman mediates between past and future on the basis of his "inspiration," where does that inspiration come from and what is its substance likely to be? Kissinger answers this question with another reference to history and a nearly circular argument. The statesman is that individual who, especially by his diplomacy, shapes history. But leadership styles are to a large extent themselves the product of historical factors. Kissinger's 19th century statesmen reflect the geopolitical position, domestic structure, and philosophic traditions of their native lands. In *A World Restored* Kissinger distinguishes between the "continental statesmanship" of Metternich, and the "insular statesmanship"of Castlereagh suggesting that the nature of the problems they faced--preserving Austrian independence from neighboring powers and revolutionary ideas, and involving an isolated and stable Britain in European affairs--required very different diplomatic approaches and leadership qualities.[43] Metternich was necessarily manipulative, Castlereagh appropriately principled. In the 20th century Kissinger tells us that leadership styles in the West, the East, and the third world are largely dictated by the power positions, philosophic principles, and domestic structures of the nations in each category.[44] For the United States in the 1950s and 1960s, the problem Kissinger saw in the quality of foreign policy leadership was not only a matter of the organizational backgrounds of many elected and appointed officials, it was also a consequence of the fact that those leaders acted in the context of American philosophic and historical experience—pragmatism, isolationism, moralism, and innocence about the use of power. Ordinary political leadership, even when it was decisive and nonbureaucratic, was still the product of national experience and character.

There is, however, a higher form of leadership. When national experience proves to be an inadequate guide to action, especially when it is threatened by a volatile international order, the statesman must transcend his national experience. Such a transcendence entails great risks since it may easily be misunderstood, repudiated, and ultimately rejected in domestic politics. The successful statesman must, therefore, educate his supporters while at the same time responding to new and dangerous realities in the world. This is an almost impossible task and those who attempt it often live tragic lives. By the criteria of transcendent statesmanship, all of the political leaders about whom Kissinger has written were failures. Metternich refused to reform the Austrian empire to make it compatible with the pressures of a democratic century. Castlereagh committed Britain to participate in a European balance of power without permanently convincing Parliament, or even his fellow cabinet ministers, that such a policy was necessary.[45] Bismarck united Germany, but created a political and diplomatic system so complex that only he could manage it.[46]

Values are less arbitrary for Kissinger than they are for Weber; they are rooted in the philosophic traditions and historical experiences of nations. But because of these roots, the role of the statesman is much more demanding. Kissinger's statesman needs more than a commanding personality and experience in public affairs; he must also understand the sources of national character and values, and be able to transcend those sources when international situations threaten vital national interests and, perhaps, survival. Where Weber separates leadership from substance, making leadership an arbitrary force in human affairs, Kissinger links statesmanship to history and makes true statesmanship practically impossible to achieve. Both agree, in any case, that statesmen will be harder to find in an increasingly bureaucratized world.

CONCLUSION

The views of Max Weber and Henry Kissinger deserve particular attention in any consideration of the bureaucratic problem in American foreign policy. Weber, perhaps the preeminent social scientist of this century, was fascinated and frightened by the bureaucratization of Germany and of western civilization which he witnessed in his lifetime. Understanding bureaucracy and its relationship to social leadership was one of the central themes in his scholarly research, and warning the world about the dangers of a bureaucratic age was one of his principal public objectives. Though speaking from another continent and another era, Weber remains an important authority for anyone seeking to understand bureaucracies or political leaders, or the relationship between them.

Henry Kissinger's observations and analysis are important for another reason. Kissinger is, of course, more than a mere observer of American foreign policy. For eight years he was the intellectual architect, the leading spokesman, and often the sole negotiator of the foreign policy of the United States. Having spent years as a critic of America's conduct in international politics, he suddenly found himself at the center of American foreign policymaking, and in the employ of a president, who for different reasons, shared Kissinger's suspicions of the foreign policy bureaucracies and was willing to permit his closest advisers to exercise an extraordinary discretion. As a result, Kissinger's academic views on the subject of bureaucracy and statesmanship can be compared to his actions in Washington and to the accounts that Kissinger and his critics give of that period in the history of American foreign policy. Those accounts vary widely and illustrate the promise, the problems and the tragedies of the political leader attempting a shape a new foreign policy in a bureaucratic age.

FOUR

Kissinger
And The Bureaucracy

Late in 1968 when Henry Kissinger agreed to serve as national security adviser to the newly elected President Nixon, he left behind his academic career and for the next eight years served two presidents as their principal adviser in foreign affairs. While in office he had ample opportunity to act on the basis of the conclusions he had reached as an analyst and critic of American foreign policy. In fact, as Kissinger explains in his memoirs, his academic research formed the only possible basis for his actions in office since "the convictions that leaders have formed before reaching high office are the intellectual capital they will consume as long as they continue in office." This occurs because there is "little time for a leader to reflect" and because policymakers "are locked in an endless battle in which the urgent constantly gains on the important."[1] Given the pace of events and the extraordinary demands on the time of national leaders, they rarely have opportunities for careful study of all, or even most, of the issues they encounter. In one of his early informal moments with the National Security Council staff, Kissinger explained that since coming to Washington he had not had a new idea, an observation with which many of his critics would readily concur.[2]

One of Kissinger's old ideas and one that was at the heart of the intellectual capital upon which he would draw was a highly developed critique of the bureaucratic character of American foreign policymaking and a conviction that the corrective for America's bureaucratic problem could only be found in the decisions and actions of those who exercised political leadership. Kissinger's first action upon receiving his appointment was to recommend the creation of a formal decisionmaking process which he would later dominate and which would enhance the power of the president in the formation of foreign policy.

THE NIXON-KISSINGER FOREIGN POLICYMAKING SYSTEM

The relationship between Richard Nixon and Henry Kissinger is one of the fascinating collaborations of individuals with different backgrounds, personalities and political philosophies who, nevertheless, are able to work together remarkably well in the execution of complicated political affairs. Like the relationships between Woodrow Wilson and Colonel House, or Harry Truman and Dean Acheson, Nixon and Kissinger had vastly different intellectual and personal experiences. A middle class California graduate of Whittier College whose political career was based on virulent anti-communism and a Jewish German immigrant who became an American citizen and a Harvard intellectual would work together to produce détentes with China and the Soviet Union and the first steps toward a comprehensive Middle East peace. Throughout their collaboration they would have a complex personal relationship which is not yet fully understood (though it is perhaps captured on the unreleased White House tapes). Kissinger who has been described as both a sycophant and a Svengali to Richard Nixon, managed to survive Watergate and continued in office under Nixon's successor, but his reputation and place in history will always be tied to the first president he served.

Since Nixon's resignation two equally erroneous views of Kissinger have emerged. Many of Nixon's persistent critics have transferred their distaste and distrust for the former president to those who served him, seeing Kissinger as the German re-incarnation of their defeated enemy and attributing to him many of the personal insecurities, intellectual shortcomings, and ideological convictions that they have always associated with Richard Nixon. Other observers are so anxious to maintain some distinction between the two that they end up crediting all the foreign policy triumphs of the early 1970s to Kissinger and all the tragedies to Nixon. Neither view is correct. And although the focus of most of what follows is on Kissinger, it should be remembered that much of the substance and style of American diplomacy in the period from 1969 to 1974 was dictated by President Nixon. In general, the two appear to have shared similar substantive conclusions about world affairs, though Nixon was often ahead of his security adviser in proposing dramatic changes, including the opening to China. In style they both preferred a system of foreign policymaking that would be centralized in the White House and dominated by the president and his personal advisers, though their reasons for preferring such a system were different.

Richard Nixon clearly wanted to be his own Secretary of State.[3] Foreign policy was his principal interest while out of office; it was reputed to be his forte; and it was the central public concern in the 1968 presidential campaign even though both major party candidates failed to offer detailed proposals for ending the war in Vietnam. Nixon appointed as his Secretary of State an old and trusted friend without experience in foreign affairs beyond a brief period of service as a delegate to the United Nations. William Rogers was, in Kissinger's blunt judgment, one of the few secretaries of state "selected because of their President's confidence in their ignorance of foreign policy."[4] The selection was evidence of Nixon's plans to personally direct foreign affairs with minimal interference from the State Department or its secretary. Nixon's reasons for wanting a weak Secretary of State were complex and included ideological, political, and psychological considerations. Ideologically he suspected the CIA and the Foreign Service of being excessively liberal and likely to disagree with his assessments of the world and his policy positions. This was, of course, largely the same Foreign Service that Kennedy eight years earlier had thought too conservative and that McCarthy even earlier has accused of being infiltrated by communists. Politically he wanted to ensure that he received the credit for the foreign policy initiatives he planned for his first term, and particularly when the 1972 election was on the horizon. And psychologically he wanted to avoid confrontations with any adviser or official representing a department likely to be hostile. This final consideration appears to have been the most important and the organization of the Nixon White House for domestic and foreign policymaking was dictated by the president's reluctance to engage in face to face policy debates unless the outcome was innocuous or preordained. As the administration developed, the growing insulation of the president from his cabinet and from all but his closest staff assistants had another explanation. According to John Erhlichman, it was important that Nixon be surrounded by people who would know that not all presidential orders could or should be obeyed.[5] His closest aides, including Kissinger, often ignored presidential instructions given in moments of anger and usually rescinded in short order. Nixon dreaded unpleasant confrontations; his staff feared irresponsible acquiescence. Both sought to limit access to the oval office.

Kissinger's role as chief foreign policy adviser to a president determined to run foreign affairs from the White House suited him about as well as it suited the president. Though Kissinger now admits that it is preferable for the Secretary of State to serve as the chief foreign policy adviser to a president, he immediately recognized that his position as national security adviser was enhanced by the selection of Rogers and by the president's disinclination to trust the Department of State or the other permanent foreign policy organizations. He acted accordingly.

In what one of Kissinger's early associates calls "the Coup d'Etat at the Pierre Hotel," Kissinger and some of the initial appointees to his NSC staff prepared a memorandum to the president-elect outlining a foreign policy decisionmaking system for the new administration.[6] Working out of the hotel in New York where Nixon maintained his transition headquarters, Kissinger and Morton Halperin, formerly a Defense Department official in the Johnson administration and later the author of books on bureaucratic politics, devised a formal plan for foreign policy decisionmaking. Modeled after the organization of the NSC under Eisenhower, the plan called for the creation of a series of interdepartmental committees chaired by assistant secretaries of state or comparable representatives from other departments. These committees would report to a Review Group chaired by the national security adviser who would be responsible for assembling options and information to be presented to the president and the National Security Council.

The Review Group was intended to be a replacement for the Senior Interdepartmental Group (SIG) which had been formed in 1967, was chaired by the under secretary of state, and was composed of under secretaries from State, Defense, and Treasury, as well as the Deputy Director of the CIA, and the Chairman of the Joint Chiefs of Staff. This had been the formal structure through which foreign policy had been made during the Johnson administration. In fact, the SIG was much less important as a policymaking forum than the regular Tuesday lunches which Johnson held with a small group of his most trusted and most senior foreign and defense advisers, but dismantling the SIG and replacing it with the Review Group was seen by many at the Department of State as evidence that their claim to primacy in the coordination of foreign policy was being usurped by the NSC staff. They saw the change correctly.

In addition to the new set of committees the plan proposed by Kissinger and Halperin gave new names and formality to the paperwork processed by the National Security Council. Requests for information and analysis from the departments would be made in National Security Study Memorandums (NSSMs) ordered by the president or the NSC and assigned to the interdepartmental committees that reported to the Review Group. Presidential decisions based on these studies were to be issued as National Security Decision Memorandums (NSDMs). In general, Nixon preferred, and this system promoted, written analysis, written presentation of options, and written decisions. National Security Council meetings were, in Kissinger's experience, usually held only after the president had privately reviewed available documents and reached his conclusions about what ought to be done.[7] They were used to ratify and announce decisions, rarely as a forum to make them.

Paperwork would be all-important in the new administration, and at the center of the flow of foreign policy paperwork would be Kissinger and his staff. In such a system, especially given Nixon's distaste for face-to-face meetings, the national security adviser would be able to exercise extraordinary influence over the information and options that went to the president, and the decisions which came from him. He would, in terms of the model of bureaucratic politics, have been in an ideal position to manipulate his superior and dominate his competitors in the bureaucratic policymaking game. Later he would be accused of both.

When drafts of this proposed plan were circulated among designated cabinet officers, there was immediate criticism, but Nixon overruled all objections—or to be more accurate, deflected all objections—and issued a directive on his first day in the White House adopting the Kissinger-Halperin recommendations. The new system was immediately put into practice. Kissinger requested a large number of agency and interagency studies on fundamental foreign and defense issues. Fifty NSSMs were issued during the first three months of the administration. Many of the documents produced in response to these requests were rejected by Kissinger and his staff and sent back to the departments and agencies for further review. Deadlines were placed on important studies and the early months of the administration became a frantic period for the bureaucracy which was forced to examine and reexamine a wide range of policies simultaneously.

Though some critics charge that this early series of National Security Study Memorandums was a diversion to keep the bureaucracies preoccupied while Nixon and Kissinger planned their strategy for the first term, Kissinger defends them as genuine requests for evaluation and recommendations. Throughout his service as national security adviser Kissinger argues that he made extensive use of the foreign affairs bureaucracies whose information and expertise were indispensable to his deliberations and actions, even if the bureaucrats providing this assistance did not always know what it was Kissinger was thinking or doing. Herein lies Kissinger's preference for a centralized decisionmaking system. Kissinger did not completely distrust the State Department or the other foreign policy agencies, though he freely joined in the denegration of them that was common practice among senior Nixon White House aides. He did believe that the departments were ill-equipped to make decisions and that they were more inclined to stifle political leadership than to serve it. Evaluating the role of the CIA in foreign policymaking Kissinger observes in his memoirs that its "analysts were only too aware that no one has ever been penalized for not having foreseen an opportunity, but that many careers have been blighted for not predicting a risk."[8] Kissinger did not fear face-to-face confrontations with people with whom he disagreed and was, in fact, one of the few members of the

Nixon White House staff who regularly met with "enemies" in the media and academic community. He used the bureaucracies as a source of information about vital international issues without a sacrificing of presidential discretion and without an obligation to make policy by interagency consensus. He wanted the maximum realm for personal choice in a policymaking environment where circumstance and bureaucratic practice almost always tended to reduce the opportunities for leaders to act.

Nixon and Kissinger achieved their objective of establishing White House control over the making of foreign policy, but they were not able to do so merely by changing the formal procedures for reporting and coordinating foreign policy. Those procedures were augmented by a mode of operation that was occasionally bizarre and often controversial. The decisions made at the Pierre Hotel were not a coup; they were a first assault on the bureaucratic policymaking status quo, followed by others which were more important.

As the administration evolved, the Nixon-Kissinger foreign policymaking system became less systematic and was increasingly characterized by secret deliberations. Kissinger went from coordinating department and agency reports, to providing the president with independent staff work and advice, to acting as his principal representative in a series of sensitive foreign negotiations. None of this was planned during the transition in late 1968, but it clearly followed from the president's attitude toward the permanent government and his desire to conduct foreign policy from the White House.

One of the extraordinary features of the Nixon-Kissinger collaboration was the degree to which important matters, and especially the opening to China, were kept secret from the American public, from the Congress, and from the permanent departments. This was done in part to satisfy foreign apprehensions about premature release of sensitive information, but only in part. Inordinate secrecy probably had more to do with domestic than with foreign apprehensions. It is an understatement to say that Nixon wanted to prevent leaks; his administration fell largely because of his overreaction to the publication of classified material. But even admitting Nixon's mania about the prevention of unauthorized disclosures, it must be acknowledged that the president had good reason to suspect that if controversial information was widely known in the bureaucracy, it would promptly appear in print. Throughout his first term, Nixon led a government and a nation deeply divided over Vietnam and the goals of American foreign policy. It is difficult to separate Nixon's paranoia about leaks from a legitimate concern for national security in a turbulent era, but both were surely present.

Unfortunately excessive secrecy, rather than preventing leaks, may have increased their frequency and seriousness. Those excluded from the policymaking process often had no way of knowing whether the release of particular information would be damaging to the administration or not, or may have felt that they had no other way of getting their opinions heard in the White House except through the pages of the *Washington Post*. Once it became clear that important foreign policy issues were not being decided by, or even with, the Secretary of State and his cabinet colleagues, demoralized employees of the permanent departments had little reason to be loyal to the administration or to protect secrets once they became known. Junior members of Kissinger's staff unaware of all his activities or unhappy about particular policy decisions were also sources for White House plumbing problems. To some degree, Nixon's fears of bureaucratic sabotage proved to be a self-fulfilling prophecy.

Though the prevention of leaks is most often mentioned as the reason for maintaining secrecy in the formulation of Nixon's foreign policy, there were other political considerations which may have been equally important. Secret deliberations about radical policy changes and secret negotiations with foreign governments were ideal script material for dramatic presidential television appearances. These announcements usually produced considerable political impact. The announcement of the president's trip to China, of the SALT breakthrough, and of the various negotiations with the North Vietnamese surprised and disarmed Nixon's critics, dominated the news, and fascinated the public. Though Nixon personally enjoyed the opportunity to confound his opponents, these announcements were also politically useful for a president who was not supported by a large majority in the Congress, who needed ways of appealing directly to the nation, and who needed foreign policy triumphs to compensate for the unpopularity of the continuing Vietnam war. Secrecy, if maintained until the proper political moment, was good public relations as well as plausible precaution in a leak-prone administration.

The secrets kept by Nixon and Kissinger about selected foreign policy initiatives could not have been kept from the public, or the bureaucracy, without the creation of back-channel lines of communication. These channels often involved elaborate intergovernmental subterfuge in which military and intelligence officers provided communications facilities to the White House for the processing of messages never seen by any of their superiors. Many Nixon appointees were encouraged to use these channels to make private reports to the White House which their superiors would never see.[9]

Gradually back-channels became the conduit for messages to various world leaders and foreign capitals, often exchanged without knowledge of the Department of State or other departments and agencies. Not only were the contents of messages restricted to White House use, even the existence of back-channels was unknown to responsible officers in the departments and agencies. Gerard Smith, the Director of the Arms Control and Disarmament Agency and the chief negotiator of the SALT I agreements, did not know that Kissinger was regularly communicating with Soviets about arms limitations until the head of the Soviet SALT delegation began responding to negotiating proposals which Smith knew nothing about.[10] Back-channel communications were not invented by the Nixon administration, but they were used by Nixon and Kissinger to a degree unprecedented in recent presidencies. They were needed to maintain secrecy about pending White House decisions and they were essential once Kissinger became the principal American negotiator dealing directly, privately, and secretly with the People's Republic of China, the Soviet Union, and North Vietnam.

Many presidents have had personal assistants carry out diplomatic missions, many have preferred to conduct international negotiations themselves at conferences and summits, but none have entrusted as many important and delicate international assignments to a White House aide as Nixon entrusted to Kissinger. Kissinger's domination of the foreign policy bureaucracies was, in the final analysis, not based on his central position as the coordinator of policymaking committees or his control of the paperwork flowing into and out of the oval office. It was based on the realization, that grew throughout Nixon's first term, that Kissinger was a surrogate Secretary of State who alone was consulted by the president on all foreign policy questions and who, in back-channels and secret meetings, conducted the important administration negotiations.

Not much changed when Kissinger was appointed Secretary of State in the fall of 1973. When he spoke to the American delegation at the United Nations shortly after he had been named to succeed Rogers, Kissinger explained, "I don't know the international significance of my appointment as Secretary of State, but domestically it represents the normalization of relations between the White House and the Department of State."[11] Kissinger's new position did end some of the more embarrassing and petty personal and institutional bickering between the president's staff and the Foreign Service, but it did not radically change the way policy was made.

Kissinger brought several members of his NSC staff with him to the Department of State and he continued to rely on a relatively small group of assistants and advisers. He still used back-channel communications not widely circulated within the bureaucracies, and he still acted without broad consultation within the government on a number of issues. He remained the president's principal foreign policy adviser, the administration's leading foreign policy spokesman, and the chief negotiator of important administration foreign policy initiatives. If anything, he carried out all of these functions more independently at State than he had in the White House, since his appointment coincided with Nixon's growing political weakness and psychological withdrawal as a result of Watergate.

For the remaining months of Nixon's presidency and for the early months under President Ford, Kissinger was both Secretary of State and national security adviser. The destruction of a president trapped in a political scandal which eventually forced his resignation and the ascension to the presidency of a former congressman without foreign policy experience gave Kissinger extraordinary opportunities to direct the policymaking process. Unfortunately, that same combination of events radically reduced the effectiveness of any American actions in international affairs regardless of who directed them. Kissinger's personal power grew in response to a vacuum created by Watergate, but that vacuum could never be filled by a presidential adviser or even by a cabinet secretary, and many of the controversial foreign policy initiatives of the first Nixon administration were abandoned or left incomplete as a result of the turbulent domestic politics of Nixon's decline and fall.

The Nixon-Kissinger foreign policymaking system did not survive the Watergate era. Kissinger's dual appointment as Secretary of State and national security adviser ended when President Ford asked him to give up his White House post as part of a series of midterm cabinet changes that also brought new secretaries to the departments of Defense and Treasury whose advice the new president regularly sought on foreign policy questions. More importantly, the Congress increasingly asserted its prerogatives on a variety of international issues significantly restricting the discretion of the president to respond to situations in Southeast Asia, Africa, and elsewhere, and making secret diplomacy in these areas virtually impossible. Hearings on the excesses of the CIA during the Nixon administration, and during previous administrations, brought new legislation governing the intelligence community and further reduced the means available to presidents wishing to influence foreign events. An increasingly cynical and voracious investigative press, which had helped to uncover the Watergate and intelligence scandals, became more aggressive as a result of these successes and further reduced the likelihood that important negotiations could be conducted in secret. By the time of the 1976 elections the Nixon-Kissinger system of foreign policymaking existed only as an issue frequently used by candidates on both the right and the left in their attacks on President Ford and his predecessor.

KISSINGER AND HIS CRITICS

The critics of how foreign policy was made during the Nixon administration are a varied lot including Republicans and Democrats, students of government organization and theorists of international politics, former Kissinger staff assistants and investigative journalists. In one sense the group includes Kissinger himself who freely admits in his memoirs that much of the personal rivalry between the national security adviser and the Secretary of State during the Nixon years was unpleasant, unproductive, and unnecessary. Kissinger also admits that the centralization of foreign policymaking in the White House had its disadvantages and that ideally a president's senior and most trusted foreign policy adviser should be the Secretary of State.[12] These caveats aside, Kissinger defends the style of decision-making and diplomacy during his years in office, and often does so vigorously. His critics are no less vigorous.

It is difficult to categorize the attacks on Kissinger's handling of American foreign affairs. They cover the political spectrum and run the gamut from the ridiculous to the subversive. Phyllis Schlafly and Chester Ward, the authors of *Kissinger on the Couch*, believe that the former national security adviser must have been "some kind of nut or something," and their evident distaste for the policies he pursued frequently degenerates into dubious speculations about his sanity.[13] Seymour Hersh, in a thoroughly researched account of Kissinger's role in the Nixon White House, describes him as an ambitious operator who simultaneously cultivated both the Democratic and Republican presidential candidates in 1968 and willingly paid whatever price was necessary for the power he craved.[14] As Hersh tells it, the price was high.

Between Schlafly and Hersh are a number of academic critics, including several theorists of bureaucratic politics, who find fault with various aspects of the Nixon-Kissinger foreign policymaking system without directly questioning Kissinger's mental health or moral character. Most of these critiques focus either on the abuse of power permitted by the policymaking apparatus of the Nixon White House or on the obstacles it created for the making of effective foreign policy. Both subjects deserve careful consideration.

Abuse of power was, of course, the major political indictment against the entire Nixon administration. It led to the first serious presidential impeachment hearings in a hundred years and eventually to Nixon's resignation. The Watergate investigations did not directly involve Kissinger, but controversy remains about the extent of his participation in the actions which led to Nixon's fall. Seymour Hersh believes that there should be no controversy and claims to have documented Kissinger's complicity in the Watergate White House. His evidence, based largely on the testimony of Kissinger detractors, has not, however, been sufficient to produce a final public verdict. Whatever Kissinger's personal role in the abuses of power which led to Nixon's resignation, it is clear that the foreign policymaking system he created did nothing to prevent such abuses. The secrecy surrounding foreign policy initiatives in the Nixon White House was strict. It sometimes prevented the exercise of constitutional checks and public examination of White House actions and may have facilitated violations of individual civil liberties. Two incidents frequently cited by critics of the Nixon-Kissinger foreign policymaking system—the secret bombings of Cambodia and the wiretapping of members of Kissinger's staff—illustrate the kinds of abuses which the concentration of power in the White House is supposed to have permitted.

Early in the Nixon presidency a decision was made to initiate B-52 bombing missions against targets in Cambodia. This was done in response to new attacks by the North Vietnamese and Viet Cong and as a substitute for a resumption of bombing in the North. Pentagon planners had long been interestsed in destroying the elusive Viet Cong headquarters and supply depots located in Cambodia. Extraordinary care was taken to insure that these missions would be kept secret, including the creation of false military reporting procedures which indicated that the attacks involved South Vietnamese rather than Cambodian targets. Despite these efforts, the *New York Times* accurately reported on the raids shortly after they began. The secret bombing of Cambodia was thus secret only for those who did not read the *New York Times*. In the months that followed the Nixon administration denied media reports about the bombing campaign and the false reporting procedures were used until February of 1971. Bombing missions in Cambodia continued until the middle of 1973 when they were finally suspended by an act of Congress. Between 1969 and 1971 official denials that Cambodia was the target of systematic bombing raids made it difficult for either the Congress or the public to evaluate these actions and exercise their legitimate roles in the making and evaluation of foreign policy.

Kissinger defends the secret bombing by pointing to the acquiescence and indirect encouragement of the Cambodian leader, Prince Norodom Sihanouk, and to the diplomatic advantages in not forcing either the Cambodians or the North Vietnamese to acknowledge the raids.[15] In 1969 much of eastern Cambodia along the border with South Vietnam was under the control of the North Vietnamese who were supplying and supporting the Khmer Rouge in addition to using Cambodian territory as a staging area for operations in South Vietnam. Cambodia's neutrality in the war in Southeast Asia was respected by neither the North Vietnamese nor the Americans. Sihanouk, who lost his throne in 1970 and went into exile has made contradictory pronouncements about the bombings. Some, like those quoted by Kissinger, suggest that he welcomed the attacks on the foreigners who first occupied his country; others express his opposition.[16]

William Shawcross believes that the bombings played a role in Sihanouk's fall by forcing the North Vietnamese and the indigenous rebels they supported to move deeper into Cambodia, producing the crisis which led to the 1970 coup and eventually to the tragic triumph of the Khmer Rouge.[17] Shawcross is probably correct when he suggests that Cambodia was a "sideshow" for Nixon and Kissinger who were more interested in ending the Vietnam war and pursuing détentes with China and the Soviet Union. He exaggerates, however, when he suggests that Nixon and Kissinger were responsible for all the freakish consequences which made the Cambodia "sideshow" of the 1970s such a hideous historical spectacle. Whatever effects the B-52 raids had, Cambodian neutrality would have faced serious challenges in the 1970s from the ravages of its internal revolutionaries and the ambitions of its militarist neighbor.

One of the obvious disadvantages of secret decisionmaking is that it forces political leaders to accept full responsibility for decisions which lead to disaster. Shawcross is at least correct in blaming Nixon and Kissinger for the failure of the Cambodian bombing to do any good, even if he goes too far in blaming them for most of the evil that visited that part of the world. It should, however, be acknowledged that the decision to bomb Cambodia belongs to a broader pattern of military and presidential policies throughout the war in Southeast Asia which were overly optimistic about the ability of air attacks to win diplomatic concessions or military victories. The greater tragedy is not that Nixon and Kissinger used illegitimate power in ordering the bombing of Cambodia, but that they squandered their legitimate power on the continuation of a flawed strategy in a lost war.

Seymour Hersh sees this tragedy as the supreme duplicity of the Nixon White House. He places the Cambodian decision in a broader context and argues that, for Nixon, the announced and enacted policies of Vietnamization and negotiated settlement were a cover for secret plans to win the war, or at least to use force as the principal means of securing a satisfactory settlement. This is part of his "madman" theory of Nixon's foreign policy which portrays Nixon as intentionally reckless about the use of military power, including nuclear weapons, in a constant effort to intimidate his foreign adversaries.[18] As for Kissinger, Hersh describes his diplomacy as a cynical attempt to secure a "decent interval" between American withdrawal and the inevitable fall of South Vietnam.[19] Hersh no doubt reports accurately on comments made by the president and his security adviser, but he reads too much into the private conversations reported to him by his various sources. In his taste for the "mad" moments in the president's conversation and the morose musings of his adviser, Hersh misses the obvious. Nixon and Kissinger were seriously searching for an honorable withdrawal from Vietnam. If there was a secret plan for winning the war it was a presidential delusion; and if face saving was the sole objective of the secret Paris peace talks, Kissinger was an inept negotiator.

The Nixon-Kissinger decisionmaking system gives some legitimacy to Hersh's investigative procedures, since a system that depends on two central decisionmakers enhances the significance of everything they say and do. But while Hersh has uncovered tantalizing conversations within the White House, he has not provided a convincing explanation of American policy in Southeast Asia. His answers are too simple and sinister; they obscure the full tragedy of Vietnam and the extent to which there were no easy exits from that war. American foreign policy in Southeast Asia, whatever its failings, does not constitute a clear case of abuse of power. The wiretaps do.

The accusation that Nixon and Kissinger engaged in illegal activites and that they violated the constitutional rights of individuals in the pursuit of foreign policy goals is perhaps the most serious charge brought against them. It is one that is likely to remain unresolved for some time to come. Morton Halperin, who assisted Kissinger in the creation of the centralized foreign policymaking system adopted by Nixon, left the National Security Council staff during the first year of the administration. Both before and after his departure, his home phone was tapped and summaries of his private conversations were provided to the White House by the FBI. He was not the only member of the NSC staff subjected to secret surveillance; nor were these wiretaps, ordered by the Nixon White House and intended to gather information about leaks of classified information, limited to NSC staff members. Telephones belonging to reporters, to White House speechwriters, and to the personal assistants to cabinet officers were also tapped in efforts to uncover the sources of unauthorized foreign policy disclosures. The wiretaps apparently produced no incriminating evidence against any of those who were investigated even though some of the wiretaps were maintained for a considerable period of time.

Kissinger claims that his only role in this matter was to provide the names of individuals who had had access to documents and information leaked to the press.[20] This is contested by other sources and is the subject of lawsuits that have not yet been settled. Regardless of Kissinger's personal involvement, it is clear that the Nixon White House ordered the surveillance of individuals inside and outside the administration in numbers, and for lengths of time, wholly out of proportion to the seriousness of the original disclosures. National security may have been the legitimate reason for some of this activity; later it became the rationalization for most of it. The fact that national security decisionmaking was restricted to a small circle of individuals, and that one of those individuals was Richard Nixon, contributed to this abuse of power. Secrecy was an important element of the Nixon-Kissinger foreign policymaking system and its protection was particularly important to Nixon who thought that the foreign policy initiatives of his administration would dramatically change world politics and be the foundation of his political reputation. Nixon's preoccupation with secrecy was not the product of the system by which foreign policy was made, but a highly centralized staff run by White

House assistants, who depended directly and completely on presidential favor, was not likely to provide an effective check on excessive presidential fears or on illegal presidential directives. It is with some justification that Kissinger admits in his memoirs that the White House ordered wiretaps were "the part of my public service about which I am most ambivalent."[21]

If Kissinger's unusual ambivalence suggests that there may be substance in the wiretap charges, he expresses no such doubts in response to the other major accusation against the Nixon-Kissinger foreign policymaking system. Most of the academic critics of Kissinger's foreign policy are less concerned with whether or not he abused power and more interested in how he used the enormous power he possessed. They often argue that Kissinger and the foreign policymaking system he instituted failed to make effective policy.

Many observers find Kissinger's management of foreign affairs to be dangerously inefficient. A centralized White House or State Department staff responsible for foreign policy depends on a small number of people and obviously has a limited capacity to deal with the vast array of issues in international politics. If such a system takes on a small agenda, it is likely to ignore important problems; if it takes on a large agenda, it is bound to treat some matters superficially.

If a small centralized foreign policy staff can deal only with a small number of issues, but manages to select and concentrate its energies on those issues which are most important, then its limited capacity is not a disabling disadvantage. A case could easily be made that the foreign policy activities of the Nixon White House—the China opening, détente, the Vietnam negotiations, and strategic arms limitation—provide a fair list of the central questions on the international agenda in the period from 1968 to 1974. I. M. Destler argues to the contrary that not only were there limitations to the time and capacity of Nixon White House foreign policy staffers, but there was also bad judgment concerning how that time and capacity should be spent.[22] Crucial foreign policy matters, particularly in international economics, were ignored by Nixon, Kissinger and the NSC staff because the president and his national security adviser had no interest in these subjects and because the White House had no time or expertise to deal with them. Roger Morris, who worked for some time on the Kissinger NSC, claims that his boss had little knowledge or interest in African affairs or the Third World in general.[23] As a result, serious mistakes were made during the Nigerian civil war and in the Cyprus dispute when neither the State Department nor the White House took effective action. Kissinger's reportedly cavalier attitude toward Latin America is cited by one critic along with an anecdote in which Kissinger jokingly describes the South American continent to his associates as a "dagger pointed at the heart of the Antarctic."[24] It is perhaps ironic that the revival of Kissinger's career as a public servant involved a commission studying the handle of that dagger.

While it may be debatable whether President Nixon and his national security adviser gave their attention to the correct set of international problems in the late 1960s and early 1970s, it is equally debatable whether a foreign policy decisionmaking system that gave more influence to the established departments and agencies would have done a better job of agenda setting. If it is obvious now that more attention might have been given in the Nixon administration to energy and international economic policy, it would have been much harder to recognize the importance of those problems when they were emerging in the early 1970s. In any case, the State Department does not have an impressive record or reputation for identifying new international problems. Kissinger argues that one of the serious limitations in the State Department suggestions for the president's annual foreign policy message was the fact that State speech drafters failed to distinguish which issues and initiatives were really important. When asked to contribute to the speech the Department produced a laundry list of short paragraphs giving equal status and consideration to all of the policies started or advanced by the department's various subdivisions. A foreign policy-making system based on the Department of State would not automatically ensure that the most important international problems received priority.[25]

Critics of the Nixon-Kissinger foreign policymaking system generally go beyond pointing out the limited number of issues it was able to address. The fact that the staff was small also meant that there were serious limitations to the degree of expertise that the staff could possess. This lack of depth and specialized knowledge is considered to have been an important problem in the SALT I negotiations. Tad Szulc reports that "several Pentagon experts who dealt with Kissinger at the time [during the SALT negotiations] have agreed that despite his conceptual mastery of nuclear strategy, he seemed to lack even minimal technical expertise."[26] Paul Nitze, a member of the SALT delegation that met in Helsinki and Vienna, argues that because Nixon and Kissinger often ignored the SALT delegation and Washington experts in their private and back-channel negotiations, "the President and his immediate advisers were deprived of available expertise and of the ability to fine comb the relevant detail. This resulted in unnecessary difficulties, some of significant consequences, in parrying Soviet strategy and tactics."[27]

A similar criticism was made in 1976 when the House Select Committee on Intelligence evaluated the role of the intelligence community in SALT I and concluded that:

> ... in the final stages of SALT talks, U.S. negotiators did not fully consult or inform intelligence experts who had been key figures in previous treaty sessions. Only Russian technical experts were on hand. Dr. Kissinger's private talks with Soviet leaders in this period were not disseminated. Some officials assert that 'ambiguities' which plague the accords may have been the result of U.S. policymakers' self-imposed intelligence blackout at the critical moment.[28]

Kissinger defends himself against these criticisms by pointing out that during the SALT negotiations and in other back-channel negotiations there was extensive utilization of departmental expertise. The series of National Security Study Memorandums and the frequent meetings of the Verification Panel where department and agency arms control reports were reviewed, provided an education for Kissinger and his staff in the relevant details of the SALT issues. Department representatives were in this process sometimes asked to comment on "theoretical" negotiating positions which were in fact actual proposals being discussed in the back-channel. "I never negotiated," Kissinger observes in his memoirs, "without a major departmental contribution even when the department did not know what I was doing."[29] In at least some cases, those who criticize Kissinger for not consulting the experts in the bureaucracy mean that Kissinger failed to inform those experts that their advice was being sought on important points under negotiation rather than theoretical propositions. The implication in such criticism is that expert advice on actual proposals would have been different than expert advice on theoretical ones. That implication obviously calls into question the extent to which expertise is objective or essential.

The most outspoken critics of the Nixon-Kissinger style in the making of foreign policy accuse the President and his national security adviser of duplicating the problems they set out to alleviate. According to Vincent Davis the Nixon NSC was itself a substantial bureaucracy with some one hundred fifty staff members and many of the defects which students of American foreign policy attribute to large organizations. The Kissinger era NSC was, Davis argues, an organization in which information was manipulated, in which personal jealousies affected policy decisions, and in which powerful ambitions often distorted professional judgments.[30] Roger Morris reaches a similar conclusion:

> The intellectual and would-be statesman alternated with a caricature of the very qualities Kissinger had ever deplored in officialdom—neglect of issues beyond ones specialty, suspension of judgment and suppression of facts to suit the preconceptions of a less competent superior, and not least, a growing inability to see the pernicious cost of self-compromise. By midway into 1969, Henry Kissinger had become, in some measure, one more bureaucrat.[31]

The Nixon administration NSC system was inefficient, these writers suggest, for the same reasons that the permanent foreign policy organizations of the government are inefficient. Rational policy evaluation and selection, even in the relatively small Nixon White House staff, came into conflict with personal ambitions and organizational interests. In Morris' judgment, "organizational grasping played its distorting role at these upper reaches of the NSC structure no less than in the linoleumed partitions of State and Defense."[32]

Kissinger is one of the best chroniclers of the personal rivalries in the Nixon administration and often admits that these relationships had effects on policy outcomes. He was not himself above acting like the bureaucrats he criticized while a Harvard professor, and even jokes that an academic background may be excellent training for government officials who must engage in bureaucratic competition for influence.[33] But because these personal and institutional struggles were limited to a few presidential appointees and advisers, and because Kissinger usually prevailed in them, they did not play a crucial role in the formation of Nixon's foreign policy. Kissinger would probably be happy with Morris' conclusion that he was a statesman half the time, even if he was a bureaucrat the other half. Morris would not. He clearly expected more. Kissinger's greatness would have been less uncertain, Morris argues, if he had reformed the State Department instead of manipulating it. "The century's most thoughtful and practically effective critic of bureaucracy in foreign affairs, Kissinger had no taste or skill to do more than suppress it."[34] But what more could have been done? One searches in vain the pages of Morris' book for some ideas about how the making of foreign policy could be improved. He does say that he wants more "public knowledge in international affairs," and a decisionmaking system which will assure an "authentic range of specializations and advice."[35] He wants, in other words, more democracy and more expertise, but those goals are not completely compatible. Morris' own comments about American government and politics raise serious doubts about how they would be achieved. Morris sees incompetence in the permanent departments, gullibility in the press, superficiality in the Congress and decadence in the old liberal foreign policy establishment. His account of how Kissinger manipulated or dominated these forces with apparent ease leaves little hope that they could, or should, be given more of a role in international affairs.

CONCLUSION

Near the end of his account of the 1971 breakthrough in the SALT I negotiations, which involved extensive back-channel negotiations and understandable animosities between the White House and the official SALT delegation, Kissinger admits that there were problems with the way foreign policy was made in the Nixon administration. Nixon's "administrative approach," he writes in his memoirs, "was weird and its human cost unattractive, yet history must also record the fundamental fact that major successes were achieved that had proved unattainable by conventional procedures."[36]

The ultimate test of any foreign policy decisionmaking system necessarily involves an evaluation of the policies it produced. It is beyond the scope of this study and perhaps too early in the course of history to reach firm conclusions about the Kissinger era in American foreign policy. Though there is broad recognition that the opening to China was a dramatic and necessary change in the course of international affairs, the remainder of the Kissinger legacy is controversial. What can be noted now is that Kissinger offers three general responses to the critics of the foreign policymaking system he established in the Nixon White House.

The first response involves the president's personality. Nixon, in Kissinger's view, had a "powerful tendency to see himself surrounded by a conspiracy reaching even among his Cabinet colleagues."[37] He shielded himself from many of his own appointees and depended on his closest advisers who, in turn, shielded the world from the most extreme Nixon proposals. It is the president's administrative approach which Kissinger calls "weird," and while Kissinger does admit that his competition with William Rogers for dominance in foreign affairs may have been influenced by the "less elevated motives of vanity and quest for power," he usually attributes the distrust and mistreatment of staff and cabinet officers to Nixon's paranoia.[38]

A president in the late 1960s and early 1970s may well have been justifiably paranoid. Kissinger's second response to his critics is a reminder about the times during which he served. By the late 1960s Vietnam had become a bitter and divisive issue in American politics and American society. Debates about the war had degenerated into violent protests by a small minority of the population, confused frustration by the vast majority, and ineffective support from those who thought they understood its purpose. The furor over the war was part of a larger generational confrontation that had broader social and philosophic origins and brought deep political divisions into many American homes.

As Kissinger observed, this conflict had profound consequences for the conduct of government:

> The modern bureaucratic state, for all its panoply of strength, often finds itself shaken to its foundations by seemingly trivial causes. Its brittleness and the world-wide revolution of youth—especially in advanced countries and among the relatively affluent—suggest a spiritual void, an almost metaphysical boredom with a political environment that increasingly emphasizes bureaucratic challenges and is dedicated to no deeper purpose than material comfort.[39]

What happened to American society as a whole in the Nixon years happened with a vengeance to the foreign policy establishment—the lawyers, businessmen, and academics informed and interested in international affairs who had, up until Vietnam, generally shared assumptions about the world and America's role in it. When Nixon and Kissinger arrived in the White House the old foreign policy establishment was busy destroying itself and any remnants of the bipartisan foreign policy it had formulated. Many of the officials responsible for the decisions which took American troops to Southeast Asia became vehement opponents of the war. Those who continued to support it lost friends and political support. And all who had once shared common goals about American foreign policy found themselves increasingly divided and insecure. These problems obviously had an impact on the way foreign policy was made under Nixon and Kissinger and the level of distrust and bad feelings which pervaded the bureaucracies, shaped their relations with the White House and even affected the performance of Kissinger's own NSC staff.

Kissinger's final response to his critics is his simplest. How foreign policy was made in the White House or the State Department is not, in the end, very important. "Ultimately there is no purely organizational answer, it is above all a problem of leadership."[40] Though Kissinger has been a keen observer of bureaucracies and has proven himself to be an accomplished bureaucratic politician, he does not regard the organization of the government to be a decisive factor in the quality of the policies that government produces. A far more important factor is the nature of the leadership exercised by those in positions of responsibility. In the constant tension between the bureaucrat and the statesman, which is the theme in so much of his research and writing, Kissinger sees the need to pay attention to questions that go far beyond how a government is organized. Understanding Kissinger's relations with the bureaucracies in American foreign policy will be incomplete without an inquiry into the status of his statesmanship.

FIVE

Kissinger And The Dilemmas Of Statesmanship

The term statesmanship is not widely used by observers of American foreign policy. It is not found in *The American Political Dictionary* or the eight volume *Handbook of Political Science.*[1] Social scientists evidently consider statesmanship to be a value-laden term. The values with which it is laden are, however, not necessarily positive. When the word appears in the work of journalists and commentators it is, more often than not, used mockingly. A statesman is a dead politician, or one who advocates policies with which we agree. A president who travels abroad is seeking to convey a "statesmanlike" appearance, particularly if he is engaged in the very unstatesmanlike activity of running for reelection.

Henry Kissinger uses the word statesmanship throughout his memoirs and not only when referring to himself. His views on the nature of leadership in foreign affairs are important for understanding his relations with the bureaucracy and his place in American foreign policy. If Kissinger asserts that the bureaucratic problem is the absence of statesmanship, the fundamental question to be asked about his years in public service is the extent to which he provided the absent leadership he so frequently lamented.

KISSINGER AND THE NATURE OF STATESMANSHIP

From the earlier review of his academic writings, it is clear that statesmanship has been a subject of lifelong interest to Kissinger. In his memoirs and in the statements he made during and after his years in public service, Kissinger offers many observations on the nature of leadership in foreign affairs. These observations often echo the lessons he learned from the study of history, but they also reflect the lessons he learned from the making of it. Both sources need to be culled to give a full account of his views on this subject.

The first, and perhaps obvious, point to make is that for Kissinger the statesman deals with matters of state and the art of diplomacy. Kissinger sees little need for extraordinary leadership in domestic politics, and tends to regard domestic issues and institutions primarily as constraints on effective diplomacy. The problem is that domestic issues, in most regimes but particularly in democracies, are subject to extensive study, exhausting debate, and eventual compromise. According to Kissinger, these practices are impossible or inappropriate in questions of foreign affairs. Early in the first volume of his memoirs, Kissinger criticizes Lyndon Johnson because "the very qualities of compromise and consultation on which his domestic political successes were based proved disastrous in foreign policy."[2] Why is it that compromise and consultation lead to disaster? The answers to this question reveal the essential elements of what Kissinger means by statesmanship.

Issues in foreign affairs, in Kissinger's view, cannot be subjected to excessive study and discussion because international events move too quickly and the ability to control them, which is always tenuous in a world of many sovereign states, is easily lost. Kissinger repeatedly warns that the leader who fails to control events will become their prisoner. But controlling events means acting "in a fog of incomplete information,"[3] because "when the scope for action is greatest, the knowledge on which to base such action is often least; when certain knowledge is at hand, the scope for creative action has often disappeared."[4]

Kissinger would agree with Allison and Halperin that rational actor decisionmaking is impossible to achieve in foreign policymaking, but not because bureaucratic politics intervenes. The careful calculation of all alternatives and the selection of the course of action which maximizes the national interest is for Kissinger inherently impossible, with or without bureaucracies. Such decisionmaking is impossible merely because of time; the more that is invested in the study of alternatives, the greater the risk that opportunities will be lost. Thus one of Kissinger's frequent admonitions is against delay.

If delay can be disastrous, what must the statesman do in the many foreign policy emergencies that emerge? First of all, he must rely on previous study of the issues likely to arise. Kissinger explains that one of his great advantages over William Rogers in their struggle for influence in the Nixon administration was his familiarity with international relations. Rogers could command the full resources of the State Department, but he could not personally acquire the background knowledge necessary for the rapid rendering of informed advice. Nor could he correct this deficiency while Secretary of State. Because of the enormous demands on the time of senior policymakers, "high office," Kissinger observes, "teaches decision-making not substance."[5] Background knowledge is essential for responding to international situations quickly, but it is not enough.

One must also possess certain skills which Kissinger describes using two of his favorite words—nuance and intuition.

> Statesmanship requires above all a sense of nuance and proportion, the ability to perceive the essential among a mass of apparent facts, and an intuition as to which of many equally plausible hypotheses about the future is likely to prove true.[6]

Intuition is, of course, not a supernatural quality. It is a skill acquired from the study of history and the practice of diplomacy. "The art of statesmanship," Kissinger notes in agreement with DeGaulle, is "to understand the trend of history."[7] But if such an art can be aided by previous study, it is hampered by too much study at the moment of decision. The statesman must be able to discern the important elements in the ambiguous situations he constantly confronts without the luxury of ample time for discussion and debate. He must by necessity avoid extensive

consultation. He should also, in Kissinger's view, avoid compromise.

Kissinger frequently praises Nixon for the bold actions he
took, often in the face of serious international and public
opposition. In the second volume of his memoirs he explains:

> I had learned in Nixon's first term, largely under his
> tutelage, that once a great nation commits itself, it
> must prevail. It will acquire no kudos for translating
> its inner doubts into hesitation. However ambivalently
> it has arrived at the point of decision, it must pursue
> the course on which it is embarked with a determi-
> nation to succeed. Otherwise it adds a reputation for
> incompetence to whatever controversy it is bound to
> incur on the merits of the decision.[8]

This was not entirely a new lesson for Kissinger. In 1961 when he
was lecturing to a Harvard class in international relations,
Kissinger's students asked him about the early reports from the
Bay of Pigs. His response was reported to be, "Well, as long as
we're there, I don't think it would do any good to lose."[9] Nations,
unlike domestic political groups, cannot easily admit failure or
compromise on an endeavor once it has begun. Despite Kissinger's frequent references to nuance, international politics is in
some respects a crude arena where excess may be needed to
communicate and where consistency is held in high regard. In a
world of competing nations with different ideologies, traditions,
cultures and leadership styles it could hardly be otherwise. But if
nations should shun compromise once action has been taken,
they should also minimize domestic political compromise before
decisions are made.

Routine compromise and consultation typical of domestic
politics are dangerous in foreign affairs because, in Kissinger's
view, the true statesman is engaged in an enterprise that will
inevitably encounter domestic resistance. This was the lesson he
learned from his study of 19th century foreign policy and it is
one that reappears throughout his memoirs.

> Most foreign policies that history has marked highly,
> in whatever country, have been originated by leaders

who were opposed by experts. It is, after all, the
responsibility of the expert to operate on the familiar
and that of the leader to transcend it.[10]

Transcending the familiar is not easy. Kissinger records Nixon's
advice to Yitzhak Rabin shortly after he became Israel's prime
minister: "there were two paths open to him; that of the politician
taking no chances or that of the statesman prepared to run risks
for peace."[11] Risk-taking is, for Kissinger, a vital part of statesmanship and courage a necessary, if all too rare, virtue among
political leaders.[12] According to one confident, "In Kissinger's
hierarchy of values, courage and decisiveness come first."[13] Not
surprisingly, Kissinger's most extensive praise in the two volumes
of his memoirs is reserved for Anwar Sadat who did take risks for
peace and eventually paid for them with his life. If a leader is to
transcend the familiar, even for the sake of peace, he must expect
problems from the individuals and institutions responsible for
existing policies. Seeking their concurrence before hand not only
brooks delay, it also invites defeat. A bold venture proposed in a
broad political forum is likely to be stopped before it is tested.

In Kissinger's famous, and infamous, interview with Oriana
Fallici he compares himself to a western hero.

Americans, like the cowboy who leads the wagon
train by riding ahead alone on his horse, the cowboy
who rides all alone into the town, the village, with his
horse and nothing else. Maybe even without a pistol,
since he doesn't shoot. He acts, that's all, by being in
the right place at the right time.[14]

This interview is frequently analyzed for what it may inadvertently reveal about Kissinger's considerable ego, but the
metaphor of the western scout is also consistent with his
observations about statesmanship and may be his awkward
effort to translate those observations into an image Americans
could easily understand. The highest form of statesman, the
leader who transcends his time, necessarily acts alone, ahead of
the wagon train, outside the routines and normal associations of
the community.

> Great statesmen set themselves high goals...; or-
> dinary leaders are satisfied with removing frictions or
> embarrassments. Statesmen create; ordinary leaders
> consume. The ordinary leader is satisfied with amel-
> iorating the environment, not transforming it; a
> statesman must be a visionary and an educator.[15]

The visionary and the educator is also the scout precariously
riding ahead of his people and constantly in danger of being cut
off from them.

   Ultimately the leader cannot remain alone. His vision of the
future must prove to be correct, and he must convince his
constituents that he has earned their support. Despite the
obvious importance of education, Kissinger appears to believe
that reaching out for public support is better done after action
has been taken, and the consequences of a new endeavor are in
view. The leader educates with both words and deeds and the
words are often most effective after the deeds are complete. Even
then it is not always possible to secure domestic support. It is as
an educator that Kissinger finds fault in his final evaluation of
Nixon.[16] Kissinger's own preoccupation once he left office has
been the preparation of his memoirs and the defense of his
controversial legacy. Though Kissinger the educator is still active
in the public arena; Kissinger the statesman remains the subject
of serious debate.

KISSINGER AND THE PRACTICE
OF STATESMANSHIP

By Kissinger's own definition, there are two essential require-
ments for statesmanship—a vision of the future which transcends the limitations of a nation's tradition, and the willingness
to take risks to impose that vision on the chaos of events through
which policymakers encounter history.

   There can be little doubt that the Kissinger era in American
foreign policy was one that involved great risks. During his eight
years in office the United States opened relations with China,
initiated a détente with the Soviet Union, and signed a major
arms control agreement. Extensive negotiations eventually

brought an end to the Vietnam war, but not before incursions into Cambodia inflamed domestic protests and persistent bombing missions in Southeast Asia aggravated moral questions about the meaning of American participation in that war. In the Middle East, the fourth major conflict between Israel and her neighbors produced both obstacles and opportunities for new peace negotiations and indirectly contributed to a revolution in the costs of energy and the management of the international economy. If there is no shortage of risky problems and policy initiatives in the Kissinger era, the pertinent question becomes to what extent were the actions that Kissinger took while in office a manifestation of a vision which somehow transformed the traditions of American foreign policy.

The content of an individual's vision is necessarily difficult to assess, particularly after events have taken place and the temptation exists to read profound intention into fortuitous action. Nevertheless, there are important aspects of Kissinger's analysis of international affairs that are consistently emphasized in his writings both before and after his White House years, and that make it possible to describe, with some reliability, what it was he was trying to accomplish, and how his version deviated from the American tradition.

Hans Morgenthau once described the American tradition in foreign policy in terms of three styles of statesmanship:

> the realist, thinking in terms of power and represented by Alexander Hamilton; the ideological, acting in terms of power, thinking in terms of moral principles, and represented by Thomas Jefferson and John Quincy Adams; the moralist thinking and acting in terms of moral principles and represented by Woodrow Wilson.[17]

After a brief period of realist foreign policy, corresponding roughly to the first decade after the ratification of the Constitution, the United States, according to Morgenthau, abandoned realism and spent a century and a half either isolated from world politics or crusading for its reform. The isolationists, for the most part, were not protecting the United States from the very real dangers of foreign wars; they were renouncing the corruption of the old world and proclaiming the uniqueness of the American experiment. Our conquest of the north American continent was seen as a manifestation of destiny and not as an exercise in power politics. Our ventures into colonial rule in the western Pacific and the Caribbean and our participation in two world wars were accompanied by surges of moral fervor and not recognitions of the need to compete for power in the global arena.

In the end, Wilsonianism and isolationism were two sides of the same coin. Both misjudged the character of international relations and failed to come to grips with vital national interests. "Isolationism stopped short of them, Wilsonianism soared above them."[18] American foreign policy in the years after World War II, according to Morgenthau, "presents itself as a slow, painful, and incomplete process of emancipation from deeply ingrained error and of recovery of long-forgotten truths."[19]

In Morgenthau's view, transcending the American tradition is the key to successful foreign policy for the United States. Despite some progress in this regard, particularly during the Truman administration, American foreign policy in the postwar decades continues to suffer from ideological rigidities and moral crusades. In its simplest form, Kissinger's vision can be seen as a return to realism in American foreign policy, just as Carter and Reagan roughly represent returns to moralism and ideology.

The consistent pattern in Kissinger's actions as a policymaker can be found in the centrality of realistic perspectives and principles. They recur in the annual foreign policy statements he drafted during the first Nixon administration, in the speeches he gave as Secretary of State, and in his memoirs. Like Morgenthau, George F. Kennan, Reinhold Neibuhr and others of the realist school, Kissinger emphasized the relations among the major powers and the need to maintain a real and perceived balance of power.[20] Like other realists, Kissinger wanted to increase the use of diplomacy by the United States, so long as there were no idealistic assumptions that the use of force was divorced from diplomatic negotiations. Like other realists, Kissinger recognized the moral ambiguity of many necessary actions in foreign affairs and was willing to persist in temporarily unpopular enterprises if they could eventually benefit the national interest.

Kissinger's particular addition to the standard set of realist principles was a conviction that in the nuclear age cooperation with potential enemies in a series of economic, political, and arms control agreements could result in the institutionalization of common interests and the moderation of revolutionary ambitions. Thus the central policy of the Kissinger era was détente and efforts to move beyond Cold War ideological competition. Those efforts were rooted in conclusions which Kissinger had developed during his career as a scholar when he had studied the era of European stability following the Congress of Vienna, and the nature of changes in international relations which had occurred as a result of nuclear weapons. When asked by a friend in 1975 to identify his most significant accomplishment, Kissinger's immediate reply was SALT.[21] The control of nuclear arms and the need to reduce the danger of war between the United States and the Soviet Union are obvious objectives for American foreign policy. Kissinger pursued them without seeking military superiority over the Soviets or a transformation of world politics. He rejected, even rhetorically, the solutions of the right and the left to the nuclear dilemma and sought security within the context of traditional realism.

Realism was not unique to Kissinger. It had, according to Morgenthau, been the dominant mode of foreign policymaking under Washington, and it was promoted throughout the postwar era by Morgenthau and other influential observers and practitioners of American foreign policy. None of those observers or practitioners, despite their significant contributions to various policy decisions, ever had the power enjoyed by Kissinger or the opportunity he possessed to dominate the policymaking process and capture public attention. Realist principles did not, of course, provide detailed guidance for every policy decision and many who would praise the direction of foreign policy under Kissinger, would also find fault with particular policies. Nevertheless, Kissinger's vision clearly involved the transcendence of our morlistic and ideological traditions and the promotion of a realist American style in foreign affairs. In pursuit of that goal he, and the presidents he served took significant political risks in ending American isolation from China, in pursuing détente with the Soviet Union, in negotiating SALT I and in resisting growing demands for a rapid end to the war in Vietnam.

But if it is easy to see in the Kissinger era the two essential elements of statesmanship—a vision of the future and a willingness to take risks to advance that vision—it is equally evident that in the final analysis Kissinger failed. His policies were rejected by the electorate in 1980 and 1984. Kissinger explains this rejection in *Years of Upheaval* with frequent references to Watergate and speculation about what might have been achieved in a normal second Nixon administration. Détente, he argues, was never fully tested as long as normalization of economic relations with the Soviet Union was held hostage to unrealistic Senate demands for Soviet immigration reform, and as long as a weakened president could not effectively respond to provocative Soviet actions in the Middle East and Africa. The complex set of responses needed to make the linkages of détente work required an active and popular president, supported in the Congress, and able to take decisive action. As the domestic crisis deepened in Nixon's second term, Kissinger, then Secretary of State, worked hard to isolate foreign policy from the consequences of the crisis, but his success in doing so was limited because his power and popularity as an adviser could never fill the gap left by a president facing impending impeachment.

It is, of course, impossible to say what might have happened in the absence of Watergate, but many of Kissinger's critics argue that his statesmanship, even before Nixon's fall, was fatally flawed. Stanley Hoffmann contends that Kissinger's vision, his grand design for American foreign policy, was too vague and too anachronistic to succeed in the world of the 1970s. Kissinger was attempting to preserve American primacy in a world in which American power was declining and in which traditional issues of Soviet-American competition were no longer the only, or perhaps even the most important, issues on the international agenda. In a world undergoing rapid and dramatic changes Kissinger approached international relations from a 19th century perspective. "Geopolitics is Kissinger's religion—its god is the balance of power, its dogma is linkage, faith is credibility, and the high priest is a United States acting on Henry Kissinger's maxims."[22] Kissinger's preoccupation with power led, in Hoffmann's view, to serious mistakes—the needless extension of the Vietnam war to preserve credibility, the inordinate and unnecessary interference in the domestic politics of Chile, and the morally dubious decisions in the crisis over Bangladesh. Even before Watergate, Kissinger's foreign policy revealed elements which would eventually be rejected by the American public and lead to failures in a world in which regional problems could no longer be subsumed by a global balance of power strategy.

Hoffmann's attack on Kissinger is essentially rooted in Kissinger's own understanding of what the American traditions in foreign affairs are and what is likely to happen to a leader who tries to go beyond those traditions. In a way Kissinger's reputation as a statesman suffers from all of the faults that Kissinger, as a scholar, found in the careers of 19th century foreign policymakers. Like Bismarck, he created a decisionmaking system so complex that only an individual with extraordinary energies and abilities could manage it. Like Metternich, he failed to fully appreciate the importance of a new agenda in international politics, and while earning a reputation for Machiavellian manipulations saw respect for the substance of his policies decline. Like Castlereagh, he was unable to sustain domestic support for a foreign policy that challenged the experiences and expectations of his nation. Like all of them he struggled against bureaucratic resistance and domestic political restraints and after periods of triumph eventually encountered the tragic fate that so often visits those who take great chances in the public arena.

CONCLUSION

The Kissinger legacy may not be the complete tragedy that comparisons with 19th century statesmen suggest. If nothing else, the Kissinger era showed what could be done, for good or ill, by a determined president, a trusted foreign policy adviser, and a small White House or State Department staff. American foreign policymaking need not be predominantly the product of organizational process or governmental politics. It can, at least under certain circumstances and for certain periods of time, be effectively directed by our highest political leaders. It ought to be obvious that presidents and their closest advisers have the ability to dominate foreign policy, but as we saw in our review of the bureaucratic problem in American foreign policy and the literature on bureaucratic politics, there is serious doubt in many

circles that such abilities exist. But if the Kissinger era demonstrates the inherent power of presidents and their advisers to
control the foreign policymaking process, there is still a question
as to whether that power will be used by other administrations.

At the time that Richard Nixon was entering office, academic
observers of American foreign policymaking were developing
two theories to explain the origins of the increasingly divisive war
in Vietnam. The contrast between these theories revives the
central dilemma we saw in the various reform proposals that
have been made for dealing with the bureaucratic problem in
American foreign policy. One theory found fault with the
distribution of power between president and Congress and
described an imperial presidency usurping powers which the
Constitution clearly intended to be shared with the legislative
branch. The solution to this problem was to decentralize power
and to create, or recreate, a significant congressional role in
foreign policymaking. The other emerging theory in the late
1960s and early 1970s blamed the Vietnam war on the bureaucracies and the military—on their inability to provide the
president with an accurate assessment of the situation in
Southeast Asia and their unwillingness to contemplate changes
once the commitment in South Vietnam had been made. The
obvious solution to this problem was exactly the opposite of the
solution to the imperial problem. Organizational inefficiencies
and inertia could best be overcome by concentrating power in the
hands of the president and his closest advisers. But a highly
centralized White House foreign policymaking system that
would increase the chances for a coherent, consistent, and bold
foreign policy would, at the same time, aggravate complaints
about an imperial executive. This is, in essence, what happened
during the Nixon administration; though the concentration of
power over foreign policy clearly produced some dramatic
initiatives in American relations with the rest of the world, it also
produced an eventual reaction against the methods by which
those initiatives were formulated and implemented.

In the aftermath of the Kissinger era, in a nation that still
suffers from what is often called the "Vietnam-Watergate syn-
drome," it is easy to see the consequences that followed from a
rejection of Kissinger's methods. Both the Carter and Reagan
administrations have consciously avoided placing a single

individual in charge of foreign policy, though neither administration has lacked volunteers for such a position. The memoirs
of Zbigniew Brzezinski and Alexander Haig share a regret that
their respective presidents did not always act decisively or
discipline their administrations to speak on foreign policy issues
with a single voice.[23] These problems were sometimes caused by
organizational inefficiencies and bureaucratic politics; and
sometimes they reflected confusion at the highest levels of
decisionmaking as to what ought to be said and done. Both of
our recent administrations have been accused by commentators
of suffering from periods of uncontrolled bureaucratic confusion
and from periods of drift where leadership was wanting. The
combination of both problems has resulted in some serious
foreign policy setbacks in Iran, in Lebanon, in arms control, and
with our European allies. Neither Carter nor Reagan, despite
successes in particular foreign policy initiatives, has earned a
national or international reputation for effective foreign policymaking.

Even if the executive branch under Carter or Reagan had
always pursued consistent international policy objectives, it
would still have encountered resistance from a Congress no
longer willing to play a subordinate role in foreign affairs. Thus
the problems of bureaucratic foreign policymaking which are
themselves complex, have been further complicated by a re-
surgent Congress and an end to the postwar tradition of
bipartisanship. Consistency in the executive branch is no longer
a sufficient, even if it remains a necessary, requirement for
effective foreign policy. In the 1980s with an international agenda
that involves many issues which directly affect domestic constitu-
encies and with a Congress naturally reluctant to relinquish
powers it acquired in the previous decade, it is by no means clear
that the Nixon-Kissinger system of foreign policymaking could
be reestablished. But it is also clear that it has not been tried.

No president who has come to office after Richard Nixon has
had extensive experience in foreign affairs or a desire to make
foreign policy the main focus of his achievements. No senior
presidential adviser or cabinet officer since Kissinger has
enjoyed the exclusive trust of his president or the license to
dominate other organizations and actors in the foreign policymaking process. Furthermore, no recent figure in American

foreign policy, president or adviser, has had a clear set of objectives for the direction of American foreign policy. The pronouncements of over-arching goals, like the promotion of human rights or the return to the Cold War, have been compromised in practice or abandoned before approaching elections. The successes of recent administrations in foreign affairs appear to be isolated and unconnected. Under such circumstances the bureaucratic problems that have plagued postwar American foreign policy have reemerged as has attention to the play of bureaucratic politics in the making of critical foreign policy decisions.

But if power in the making of recent American foreign policy decisions is diffused, the Kissinger legacy teaches that the concentration of power in the hands of a few policymakers and a small staff would not, in and of itself, guarantee effective foreign policymaking. Unlike many of the observers and critics of the bureaucratic problems in American foreign policy, Kissinger does not believe that reforms or reorganizations will suffice, or even go very far, in alleviating the problems we face. "Ultimately . . . it is above all a problem of leadership."[24]

The important lesson to learn from Kissinger's scholarship and from his memoirs is the special significance of statesmanship in foreign affairs. Beyond the platitude that leaders make a difference, Kissinger offers at least an outline of what effective leadership in international politics entails. Certain qualities of character and intellect are essential elements of Kissinger's concept of statesmanship. They include a knowledge of history; an appreciation for the different cultures, traditions, and leadership styles which other nations bring to their foreign policies; an ability to quickly interpret complex and confusing situations; and the courage to take chances in a rapidly changing international environment. The most lasting form of statesmanship involves a recognition of the limits posed by one's own national traditions and a willingness to reshape or transcend those traditions in pursuit of a more stable and more secure world order.

What Kissinger has to say about the subject of statesmanship is by no means the last word. It comes much closer to being the first words on a neglected and important topic. His observations need to be tested, not only against his own performance in office, but also in careful examination of the history of international politics and in a serious reflection on contemporary international issues. Kissinger's version of statesmanship is particularly weak on the problem of building consensus and support for actions in the international arena. He clearly recognizes the need for such support, but in the balance that must be struck between innovation and institutionalization and between creativity and consensus, Kissinger consistently emphasizes the former at the expense of the latter. This is a reflection of his understanding of the central problem in a bureaucratic age and the particular defect of American foreign policymaking, and there may be good reasons for making the choices he makes. But if Lyndon Johnson's problem was a tendency to make foreign policy decisions on the basis of compromise and consultation, Richard Nixon's problem, and by implication Henry Kissinger's, was a tendency to isolate himself and to depend on dramatic successes to win popular approval. That strategy worked well, especially in the period before the 1972 election, but it made possible, and perhaps inevitable, the rapid decline in public support which accompanied reversals in domestic and international fortunes.

The Kissinger understanding of statesmanship may also be faulted for its vague account of the qualities necessary for effective decisionmaking. He does provide more than mere maxims, but the repetitive references to nuance, proportion and intuition are insufficient explanations of a vital phenomena. Kissinger can be praised for taking the examination of decisionmaking beyond the stilted calculations of cost-benefit analysis, or the abstract theories of gaming, or the limited perspective of bureaucratic politics. For Kissinger the foreign policy decisionmaker is at once engaged in an intellectual, a psychological, a political, and an emotional process, but the very complexity of the process cries out for more systematic analysis.

It is perhaps unfair to demand more analysis from someone who has already written a few thousand pages of memoirs and enough academic books and articles to earn tenure at Harvard. But the most lasting Kissinger legacy may not be the particular policies he championed as much as the issues he raised about the making of American foreign policy. Those issues are currently overshadowed by other concerns. To speak favorably about the way that Henry Kissinger and Richard Nixon went about making foreign policy will not be fashionable as long as there are ripples in the wake of Watergate. To defend secrecy and back-channels and the concentration of foreign policymaking power in the hands of a single presidential adviser will never be wholly acceptable in a democracy. But to draw our attention away from the organizations and processes that contribute to the formation and implementation of critical policies and to focus instead on the character and behavior of our highest officials is an important contribution. Kissinger urged that redirection of attention when he was a scholar, he worried whether an increasingly bureaucratized America could produce the leadership qualities he regarded as essential when he served as an adviser and critic of the administrations in the 1950s and 1960s, and he attempted while in office to act on the principles which he had earlier preached. Whether or not one concludes that Henry Kissinger successfully practiced the statesmanship he prescribed may be less important than the contribution he has made to our understanding of the deeper nature of the bureaucratic problem in American foreign policy.

Notes

CHAPTER ONE

1. I.M. Destler, *Presidents, Bureaucrats and Foreign Policy* (Princeton, New Jersey: Princeton University Press, 1972), p. 2.
2. Quoted in, Graham Allison, *Essence of Decision* (Boston: Little Brown, 1971), p. 86.
3. Robert F. Kennedy, *Thirteen Days* (New York: Norton, 1969), p. 95.
4. Richard Neustadt, *Presidential Power: The Politics of Leadership* (New York: Wiley, 1960), p. 9.
5. John Krizay, "Clientitus, Corpulence and Cloning at State; The Symptomatology of a Sick Department,"*Policy Review* (Spring 1978).
6. Destler, pp. 159-60.
7. Ellis Briggs, *Farewell to Foggy Bottom* (New York: McKay, 1964), p. 166.
8. Henry M. Jackson, editor, *The National Security Council* (New York: Praeger, 1965), p. 67. This book is an edited version of testimony taken by the Subcommittee on National Security Machinery of the Senate Committee on Government Operations.
9. Quoted in, John Franklin Campbell, *The Foreign Affairs Fudge Factory* (New York: Basic Books, 1971), p. 190.
10. Smith Simpson, *Anatomy of the State Department* (Boston: Beacon Press, 1967).
11. Jackson, p. 81.

12. George F. Kennan, "America's Administrative Response to its World Problems," *Daedalus*, Vol. 87, No. 2 (Spring 1958), p. 24. For a similar argument see Louis Halle, *Dream and Reality: Aspects of American Foreign Policy* (New York: Harper and Brothers, 1958), pp. 313-15.
13. Richard Holbrooke, "The Machine That Failed," *Foreign Policy,* No. 1 (Winter 1970-71), p. 72.
14. Charles Frankel, *High on Foggy Bottom: An Outsider's Inside View of the Government* (New York: Harper & Row, 1968), pp. 29-30.
15. Campbell, p. 7. This was also a theme in "Toward a Modern Diplomacy," a report to the American Foreign Service Association by its Committee on Career Principles, AFSA, 1968. A similar argument is made in the Murphy Commission Report and Graham Allison and Peter Szanton, *Remaking Foreign Policy* (New York: Basic Books, 1976).
16. Arthur M. Schlesinger, Jr., "Roosevelt as Chief Administrator," in Francis Rourke, editor, *Bureaucratic Power in National Politics* (Boston: Little Brown, 1978), 3rd ed., pp. 257-69.
17. Quoted in William I. Bacchus, *Foreign Policy and the Bureaucratic Process* (Princeton, New Jersey: Princeton University Press, 1974), p. 288.
18. John Kenneth Galbraith, "Plain Lessons of a Bad Decade," *Foreign Policy,* No. 1 (Winter 1970-71), p. 39.
19. Graham Clayton, War College speech reported in the *New York Times* March 28, 1978. For a general treatment of this problem see, Guy Benveniste, *The Politics of Expertise* (San Francisco: Boyd & Fraser, 1977).
20. These arguments are frequently mentioned in discussions of the arms race or Vietnam. Two examples would be: Graham Allison and Frederic Morris, "Armaments and Arms Control: Exploring the Determinants of Military Weapons," in Franklin A. Long and George W. Rathjens, eds., *Arms, Defense Policy and Arms Control* (New York: Norton, 1976), pp. 99-129 and James C. Thomson, "How Could Vietnam Happen?" in Morton Halperin and Arnold Kanter, eds., *Readings in American Foreign Policy* (Boston: Little Brown, 1973), pp. 98-110.
21. Theodore Sorensen, *Kennedy* (New York: Harper, 1965), p. 309.
22. Richard Barnet, *Roots of War* (New York: Atheneum, 1972), p. 137.
23. *Ibid.*, p. 137 and 97.
24. Galbraith, p. 40.
25. Francis E. Rourke, *Bureaucracy and Foreign Policy* (Baltimore: The Johns Hopkins University Press, 1972), p. 47.
26. Comments by Richard Falk in Erwin Knoll and Judith Nies McFadden, eds., *American Militarism 1970* (New York: Viking Press, 1969) p. 66.

27. William D. Leahy, *I Was There* (New York: Whittlesey House, 1950), p. 441.
28. Quoted in, John P. Leacacos, *Fires in the In Basket: The ABCs of the State Department* (Cleveland: World Publishing Co., 1968), p. 362.
29. Robert L. Rothstein, *Planning Prediction and Policymaking in Foreign Affairs* (Boston: Little Brown, 1972), p. 33.
30. Theodore H. White quoted in, Arthur Schlesinger, Jr., *A Thousand Days* (Boston: Houghton Mifflin, 1965), p. 420.
31. Krizay, p. 49.
32. William A. Bell, "The Cost of Cowardice: Silence in the Foreign Service," in Charles Peters and Timothy J. Adams, eds., *Inside the System* (New York: Praeger, 1970), p. 221.
33. *Ibid.*, p. 223.
34. Schlesinger, *A Thousand Days*, p.414.
35. Quoted in, Destler, p. 69.
36. Leacacos, p. 433.
37. Quoted in, Leonard White, *The Federalists* (New York: Macmillan, 1948), p. 129.
38. Krizay, pp. 43-46.
39. Richard Betts, "Analysis, War and Decision: Why Intelligence Failures are Inevitable," *World Politics*, Vol. XXXI, No. 1 (October 1978).
40. Simpson, pp. 232-35.
41. Allison and Szanton, p. 15.
42. C. Wright Mills, *The Power Elite* (New York: Oxford University Press, 1956).
43. Galbriel Kolko, *The Roots of American Foreign Policy* (Boston: Beacon Press, 1969), p. 17.
44. *Ibid.*, p. 4.
45. Martin Weil, *A Pretty Good Club: The Founding Fathers of the U.S. Foreign Service* (New York: Norton, 1978).
46. *Ibid.*, p. 61.
47. I. M. Destler, "Can One Man Do?" *Foreign Policy*, No. 5. (Winter 1971-72).
48. Destler, *Presidents, Bureaucrats and Foreign Policy*, p. 16.

CHAPTER TWO

1. Graham T. Allison and Morton Halperin, "Bureaucratic Politics: A Paradigm and Some Policy Implications," *World Politics* Vol. 24 (Spring 1972), pp. 40-80.
2. Michel Crozier, *The Bureaucratic Phenomenon* (Chicago: University of Chicago Press, 1964), p. 3.

3. For a detailed description of the rational actor model see, Graham T. Allison, *Essence of Decision* (Boston: Little Brown, 1971), pp. 10-38.
4. Henry M. Jackson, *The National Security Council* (New York: Praeger, 1965), p. 78.
5. Allison, *Essence of Decision*, pp. 101-43.
6. *Ibid.*, p. 125.
7. *Ibid.*, pp. 185-244.
8. Allison and Halperin, "Bureaucratic Politics."
9. Morton Halperin, *Bureaucratic Politics & Foreign Policy* (Washington, D.C.: Brookings, 1974).
10. *Ibid.*
11. See Stephen D. Krasner, "Are Bureaucrats Important? (Or Allison Wonderland)," *Foreign Policy* No. 7 (Summer 1972). Robert J. Art, "Bureaucratic Politics and American Foreign Policy: A Critique," in John E. Endicott and Ray W. Stafford, eds., *American Defense Policy* (Baltimore: The Johns Hopkins University Press, 1977) 4th ed., pp. 240-53.
12. Graham T. Allison and Peter Szanton, *Remaking Foreign Policy* (New York: Basic Books, 1976). I.M. Destler, *Presidents Bureaucrats and Foreign Policy* (Princeton, N.J.: Princeton University Press, 1972).
13. Allison and Szanton, pp. 120-40.

CHAPTER THREE

1. From a 1909 speech before Verein fur Sozialpolitik, quoted in, J.P. Mayer, *Max Weber and German Politics* (London: Farber & Farber, 1943), pp. 127-28.
2. Max Weber, *Economy and Society: An Outline of Interpretive Sociology* eds. Guenther Roth and Claus Wittich (New York: Bedminster Press, 1968), p. 1399.
3. The importance of responsibility in Weber's conception of politics can be seen in his essay "Politics as a Vocation," Max Weber, *From Max Weber: Essays in Sociology*, eds. H.H. Gerth and C. Wright Mills (New York: Oxford University Press, 1946), pp. 77-128.
4. Weber, *Economy and Society*, pp. 1432-33.
5. *Ibid.*, p. 1392.
6. Kissinger reaches the same conclusion in his study of Bismarck. Henry Kissinger, "The White Revolutionary: Reflections on Bismarck," *Daedalus*, Vol. 97, No. 3 (Summer 1968), pp. 888-924.
7. Weber, *Economy and Society*, p. 1400.

8. See, Wolfgang J. Mommsen, *The Age of Bureaucracy: Perspectives on the Political Sociology of Max Weber* (New York: Harper & Row, 1974), chp. III, pp. 47-71.
9. Weber, *Economy and Society*, p. 1403.
10. *Ibid.*, pp. 1403-04.
11. *Ibid.*, p. 1404.
12. *Ibid.*, p. 1405. (Emphasis in original.)
13. *Ibid.*, p. 1431.
14. *Ibid.*, p. 1438.
15. *Ibid.*
16. *Ibid.*, p. 1450.
17. *Ibid.*, p. 1439.
18. *Ibid.*, p. 1459.
19. *Ibid.*, p. 1417.
20. Henry A. Kissinger, *A World Restored: Metternich, Castlereagh and the Problems of Peace 1812-1822* (Boston: Houghton Mifflin, 1957), pp. 326-7.
21. In Kissinger's account their ability to make lasting changes in the basic values of their respective nations was much more limited. Kissinger, *A World Restored*, p. 329.
22. Henry A. Kissinger, *Nuclear Weapons and Foreign Policy* (New York: W.W. Norton, 1969), abridged edition, p. 246.
23. *Ibid.*, p. 248.
24. *Ibid.*, p. 249.
25. Henry A. Kissinger, *The Necessity for Choice: Prospects of American Foreign Policy* (New York: Harper & Brothers, 1962), p. 341.
26. Henry A. Kissinger, *American Foreign Policy* (New York: W.W. Norton, 1977), third ed., pp. 11-50.
27. *Ibid.*, p. 18.
28. *Ibid.*
29. *Ibid.*, p. 35.
30. *Ibid.*, p. 24.
31. *Ibid.*, p. 25.
32. *Ibid.*, p. 38.
33. *Ibid.*, p. 28.
34. All three combinations are used in Kissinger's work to refer to the same fundamental distinction.
35. Kissinger, *American Foreign Policy*, p. 48.
36. Max Weber, *The Theory of Social and Economic Organization*, ed. by Talcott Parsons (New York: Free Press, 1947), pp. 363-86.
37. Weber, *Economy and Society*, p. 1420.
38. Weber, "Politics as a Vocation," p. 117 and 123.
39. *Ibid.*, p. 115 and 127.
40. *Ibid.*, p. 116.

41. Henry A. Kissinger, *White House Years* (Boston: Little Brown, 1979), p. 55.
42. Kissinger, *Nuclear Weapons and Foreign Policy*, p. 247. A nearly identical statement can be found in Kissinger, *A World Restored*, p. 329.
43. Kissinger, *A World Restored*, pp. 7-40.
44. Kissinger, *American Foreign Policy*, pp. 11-50.
45. Kissinger, *A World Restored*, pp. 325-26.
46. Kissinger, "The White Revolutionary," p. 920.

CHAPTER FOUR

1. Henry A. Kissinger, *White House Years* (Boston: Little Brown, 1979), p. 54.
2. Roger Morris, *Uncertain Greatness: Henry Kissinger and American Foreign Policy* (New York: Harper & Row, 1977), p. 94.
3. There is some evidence that Nixon did not originally plan to appoint a weak Secretary of State. See Richard Norton Smith, *Thomas E. Dewey and His Times* (New York: Simon and Schuster, 1982).
4. Kissinger, p. 26.
5. John Ehrlichman, *Witness to Power* (New York: Simon and Schuster, 1982), chps. 6-7.
6. Morris, chp. 2.
7. Kissinger, p. 491.
8. *Ibid.*, p. 37.
9. Seymour Hersh, *The Price of Power* (New York: Summit Books, 1983), p. 42.
10. Gerard Smith, *Doubletalk: The Story of Salt I* (Garden City N.Y.: Doubleday, 1980), chp. 7.
11. Quoted in, William F. Buckley, Jr., *United Nations Journal* (New York: Putnam, 1974), p. 61.
12. Kissinger, p. 30.
13. Phyllis Schlafly and Chester Ward, *Kissinger on the Couch* (New Rochell, N.Y.: Arlington House, 1975), p. 11.
14. Hersh, pp. 11-24.
15. Kissinger, pp. 249-51.
16. *Ibid.*
17. William Shawcross, *Sideshow* (New York: Pocket Books, 1979).
18. Hersh, p. 53.
19. *Ibid.*, chp. 4.
20. Kissinger, pp. 252-53.

21. Henry A. Kissinger, *Years of Upheaval* (Boston: Little Brown, 1982), p. 121.
22. I.M. Destler, *Presidents Bureaucrats and Foreign Policy* (Princeton, N.J.: Princeton University Press, 1974), pp. 295-319. Also Destler, "Can One Man Do?" *Foreign Policy*, No. 5 (Winter 1971-72), pp. 28-40.
23. Morris, pp. 120-31 and 271.
24. Quoted in, Vincent Davis, "Henry Kissinger and Bureaucratic Politics," Institute of International Studies Essay Series No. 9 (1979), p. 36.
25. Kissinger, *White House Years*, pp. 158-9.
26. Tad Szulc, *The Illusion of Peace* (New York: Viking Press, 1978), p. 77.
27. Paul Nitze, "Soviet's Negotiating Style Assayed," *Aviation Week and Space Technology* Vol. 102, No. 7 (February 17, 1975), p. 43.
28. Quoted in, Szulc, p. 579.
29. Kissinger, *White House Years*, p. 149.
30. Davis, p. 25.
31. Morris, p. 106.
32. *Ibid.*, p. 110.
33. Kissinger, *Years of Upheaval*, p. 248.
34. Morris, p. 130.
35. *Ibid.*, pp. 5 and 38.
36. Kissinger, *White House Years*, p. 841.
37. *Ibid.*, p. 25.
38. Kissinger, *Years of Upheaval*, pp. 418-19.
39. Kissinger, *White House Years*, p. 66.
40. *Ibid.*, p. 39.

CHAPTER FIVE

1. Jack C. Plano and Milton Greenberg, *The American Political Dictionary* 7th ed. (New York: Holt, Rinehart and Winston, 1985). The word statesman does appear in the index of the *Handbook of Political Science*, but only in reference to Plato's dialogue of that title. Fred I. Greenstein and Nelson W. Polsby, *Handbook of Political Science* (Reading, Mass.: Addison-Wesley Publishing Co., 1975).
2. Henry A. Kissinger, *White House Years* (Boston: Little Brown, 1979), p. 18.
3. Henry A. Kissinger, *Years of Upheaval* (Boston: Little Brown, 1982), p. 448.

4. Henry A. Kissinger, *For the Record* (Boston: Little Brown, 1981), p. 284.
5. Kissinger, *White House Years*, p. 27.
6. *Ibid.*, p. 39.
7. *Ibid.*, p. 109.
8. Kissinger, *Years of Upheaval*, p. 520.
9. Quoted in, Peter Wyden, *Bay of Pigs* (New York: Simon & Schuster, 1979), p. 209.
10. Kissinger, *Years of Upheaval*, p. 445.
11. *Ibid.*, p. 1137.
12. For a discussion of Kissinger's values see, Albert Eldridge, "Pondering Intangibles: A Value Analysis of Henry Kissinger," in Dan Caldwell, ed., *Henry Kissinger, His Personality and Politics* (Durham, N.C.: Duke Press Policy Studies, 1983), chp. 3.
13. John Stoessinger, *Henry Kissinger: The Anguish of Power* (New York: W.W. Norton, 1976), p. 209.
14. Orina Fallici, *Interviews with History* (Boston: Houghton Mifflin, 1977), p. 41.
15. Kissinger, *Years of Upheaval*, p. 1208.
16. *Ibid.*, p. 1209.
17. Hans Morgenthau, "The Mainsprings of American Foreign Policy," *The American Political Science Review* Vol. XLIV, No. 4 (December 1950), p. 840.
18. *Ibid.*, p. 851.
19. *Ibid.*, p. 853.
20. John Gaddis emphasizes the similarties between Kennan and Kissinger in, John Gaddis, *Strategies of Containment* (New York: Oxford University Press, 1982).
21. Stoessinger, p. 82.
22. Stanley Hoffmann, *Dead Ends: American Foreign Policy in the New Cold War* (Cambridge, Mass.: Ballinger Publishing Co., 1983), p. 38.
23. Zbigniew Brzezinski, *Power and Principle* (New York: Farrar Straus Giroux, 1983). Alexander M. Haig, Jr. *Caveat* (New York: Macmillan, 1984).
24. Kissinger, *White House Years*, p. 39.

Bibliography

GOVERNMENT ORGANIZATION AND FOREIGN AFFAIRS

Allison, Graham T. and Peter Szanton. *Remaking Foreign Policy*. New York: Basic Books, 1976.

Bacchus, William I. *Foreign Policy and the Bureaucratic Process*. Princeton, New Jersey: Princeton University Press, 1974

Barnet, Richard. *Roots of War*. New York: Antheneum, 1972.

Briggs, Ellis. *Farewell to Foggy Bottom*. New York: McKay, 1964.

Brzezinski, Zbigniew. "Deciding Who Makes Foreign Policy." *New York Times Magazine*, (September 18, 1983).

Campbell, John Franklin. *The Foreign Affairs Fudge Factory*. New York: Basic Books, 1971.

Destler, I.M. *Bureaucrats, Presidents and Foreign Policy*. Princeton, New Jersey: Princeton University Press, 1974.

———. "Can One Man Do?" *Foreign Policy*, No. 5 (Winter 1971-72).

———. "National Security Advice to U.S. Presidents: Some Lessons From Thirty Years." *World Politics*, Vol. 24, No. 2 (January 1977).

———. "A Job That Doesn't Work." *Foreign Policy*, No. 38 (Spring 1980).

Elder, Robert Ellsworth. *The Policy Machine*. Syracuse, New York: Syracuse University Press, 1960.

Frankel, Charles. *High on Foggy Bottom*. New York: Harper & Row, 1968.

George, Alexander. *Presidential Decisionmaking in Foreign Policy.* Boulder, Colorado: Westview Press, 1980.

Garnham, David. "State Department Rigidity." *International Studies Quarterly*, No. 18 (March 1974).

_____. "Foreign Service Elitism and U.S. Foreign Affairs." *Public Administration Review*, Vol. 35 (January/February 1975).

Gelb, Leslie. "Why Not the State Department?" *The Washington Quarterly* (White Paper Special Supplement to the Autumn 1980 Issue).

Harr, John E. *The Anatomy of the Foreign Service: A Statistical Profile.* Foreign Affairs Personnel Study No. 4, Carnegie Endowment for International Peace, 1965.

Holbrooke, Richard. "The Machine That Failed." *Foreign Policy*, No. 1 (Winter 1970-71).

Johnson, Richard T. *Managing the White House.* New York: Harper & Row, 1974.

Krizay, John. "Clientitus, Corpulence and Cloning at State—The Symptomatology of a Sick Department." *Policy Review*, No. 4 (Spring 1978).

Kennan, George F. "America's Administrative Response To Its World Problems." *Daedalus*, Vol. 87, No. 2 (Spring 1958).

Leacacos, John P. *Fires in the In-Basket: The ABCs of the State Department.* Cleveland: World Publishing, 1968.

_____. "Kissinger's Apparat." *Foreign Policy*, No. 5 (Winter 1971-72).

Lucas, William and Raymond H. Dawson. "The Organizational Politics of Defense." International Studies Association, Occasional Paper No. 2, University of Pittsburgh.

McCamy, James L. *The Administration of American Foreign Affairs.* New York: Knopf, 1950.

Nelson, Michael. "The White House, Bureaucracy, and Foreign Policy: Lessons From Cambodia." *The Virginia Quarterly Review*, Vol. 56, No. 2 (Spring 1980).

Nitze, Paul. "Eight Presidents and Their Different Approaches to National Security Policymaking." Kenneth W. Thompson, editor. *The Virginia Papers on the Presidency.* Washington: University Press of America, 1979.

Price, Don K., editor. *The Secretary of State.* Englewood Cliffs, New Jersey: Prentice-Hall, 1960.

Pringle, Robert. "Creeping Irrelevance at Foggy Bottom." *Foreign Policy*, No. 29 (Winter 1977-78).

Rothstein, Robert L. *Planning Prediction and Policymaking in Foreign Affairs.* Boston: Little Brown, 1972.

Rourke, Francis E. *Bureaucracy and Foreign Policy.* Baltimore: Johns Hopkins University Press, 1972.

_____, editor. *Bureaucratic Power and National Politics*. Boston: Little Brown, 1978.

Sapin, Burton. *The Making of United States Foreign Policy*. New York: Praeger, 1966.

Simpson, Smith. *Anatomy of the State Department*. Boston: Beacon Press, 1967.

_____. *The Crisis in American Diplomacy: Shots Across the Bow of the State Department*. North Quincy, Massachusetts: The Christopher Publishing House, 1980.

Sorensen, Theodore. *Decision-Making in the White House*. New York: Columbia University Press, 1963.

United States Congress, Senate. Subcommittee on National Policy Machinery, Committee on Government Operations. *Organizing for National Security* Vols. I-IV. Washington: Government Printing Office, 1965. Selected materials from these hearings are available in Jackson, Henry, editor. *The National Security Council*. New York: Praeger, 1965.

_____. Congress. *Report by the Commission on the Organization of the Government for the Conduct of Foreign Affairs*. (Murphy Commission). Report and Appendices Vols. I-VII. Washington: Government Printing Office, 1975.

Warnick, Donald P. *A Theory of Public Bureaucracy: Politics Personality and Organization in the State Department*. Cambridge, Massachusetts: Harvard University Press, 1975.

Weil, Martin. *A Pretty Good Club: The Founding Fathers of the Foreign Service*. New York: W.W. Norton, 1978.

Wilson, Graham K. "Are Department Secretaries Really a President's Natural Enemies?" in Harry A. Bailey Jr., editor. *Classics of the American Presidency*. Oak Park, Illinois: Moore, 1980.

Yost, Charles. *The Conduct and Misconduct of Foreign Affairs*. New York: Random House, 1972.

BUREAUCRACY AND BUREAUCRATIC POLITICS

Abrahamsson, Bengt. *Bureaucracy or Participation: The Logic of Organization*. Beverly Hills, California: Sage, 1977.

Allison, Graham T. *Essence of Decision*. Boston: Little Brown, 1972.

_____. "Questions About the Arms Race: Who's Racing Whom? A Bureaucratic Perspective." John E. Endicott and Roy Stafford, Jr., editors. *American Defense Policy*. Baltimore: Johns Hopkins University Press, 1977.

Art, Robert J. "Bureaucratic Politics and American Foreign Policy: A Critique." *Policy Sciences*, Vol. 4 (1973).

Beard, Edmund. *Developing the ICBM: A Study in Bureaucratic Politics.* New York: Columbia University Press, 1976.

Beetham, David. *Max Weber and the Theory of Modern Politics.* London: George Allen, 1974.

Bendix, Reinhard. *Max Weber: An Intellectual Portrait.* Garden City, New York: Doubleday Anchor Books, 1962.

Benveniste, Guy. *The Politics of Expertise.* San Francisco: Boyd & Frazer, 1977.

Brenner, Michael J. "The Problem of Innovation and the Nixon-Kissinger Foreign Policy." *International Studies Quarterly*, Vol. 17, No. 3 (September 1973).

Caldwell, Dan. "Bureaucratic Foreign Policy-Making." *American Behavorial Scientist*, (October 1977).

Coombes, David. *Politics and Bureaucracy in the European Community.* Beverly Hills, California: Sage, 1970.

Coulam, Robert F. *Illusions of Choice: The F-111 and the Problem of Weapons Acquisition Reform.* Princeton, New Jersey: Princeton University Press, 1977.

Crozier, Michel. *The Bureaucratic Phenomenon.* Chicago: University of Chicago Press, 1964.

_____, and Samuel Huntington and Joji Watanuki. *The Crisis of Democracy.* New York: New York University Press, 1975.

Cuff, Robert D. "Wilson and Weber: Bourgeois Critics in an Organized Age." *Public Administration Review*, Vol. 38, No. 3 (May/June 1978).

Diamant, Alfred. "The Bureaucratic Model: Max Weber Rejected, Rediscovered, and Reformed." Ferrel Heady and Sybil L. Stokes, editors. *Papers in Comparative Public Administration.* Ann Arbor, Michigan: Institute of Public Administration, 1962.

Downs, Anthony. *Inside Bureaucracy.* Boston: Little Brown, 1966.

Elliot, Jaques. *A General Theory of Bureaucracy.* New York: Wiley, 1976.

Goldwin, Robert A., editor. *Bureaucrats, Policy Analysts, Statesmen: Who Rules?* Washington: American Enterprise Institute, 1980.

Halperin, Morton H. *Bureaucratic Politics and Foreign Policy.* Washington: Brookings, 1974.

_____. *National Security Policy-Making.* Lexington, Massachusetts: Lexington Books, 1975.

_____ and Graham T. Allison. "Bureaucratic Politics: A Paradigm and Some Policy Implications." *World Politics*, Vol. 24 (Spring 1972).

_____ and Arnold Kanter, editors. *Readings in American Foreign Policy: A Bureaucratic Perspective.* Boston: Little Brown, 1973.

Hermann, Charles F. "Bureaucratic Constraints on Innovation in American Foreign Policy." Charles W. Kegley Jr. and Eugene R.

Wittkopf, editors. *Perspectives in American Foreign Policy*. New York: St. Martin's Press, 1983.

Hilsman, Roger. *The Politics of Policy-Making in Defense and Foreign Affairs*. New York: Harper & Row, 1971.

Krasner, Stephen. "Are Bureaucrats Important? (Or Allison Wonderland)" *Foreign Policy*, No. 7 (Summer 1972).

Lindblom, Charles A. *The Policy-Making Process*. Englewood Cliffs, New Jersey: Prentice-Hall, 1968.

Merton, Robert K., editor. *Reader in Bureaucracy*. Glencoe, Illinois: Free Press, 1952.

Mommsen, Wolfgang. *The Age of Bureaucracy*. New York: Harper & Row, 1974.

Rosati, Jerel A. "Developing a Systematic Decision-Making Framework: Bureaucratic Politics in Perspective." *World Politics*, Vol. 33, No. 2 (January 1981).

Rourke, Francis E. *Bureaucracy, Politics and Public Policy*. Boston: Little Brown, 1969.

Rudolph, Lloyd L. and Susanne Hoeber Rudolph. "Authority and Power in Bureaucratic and Patrimonial Administration: A Revisionist Interpretation of Weber on Bureaucracy." *World Politics*, Vol. XXXI, No. 2 (January 1979).

Seidman, Harold. *Politics, Position and Power*. New York: Oxford University Press, 1975.

Selznich, Philip. *Leadership in Administration*. New York: Harper & Row, 1957.

Simon, Herbert A. *Administrative Behavior*. New York: Free Press, 1976.

Steinbruner, John D. *The Cybernetic Theory of Decision*. Princeton, New Jersey: Princeton University Press, 1974.

Weber, Max. *From Max Weber*. H.H. Gerth and C. Wright Mills, editors. New York: Oxford University Press, 1946.

_____. *The Theory of Social and Economic Organization*. Talcott Parsons, editor. New York: Free Press, 1947.

_____. *Basic Concepts in Sociology*. H. P. Secher, translator. New York: Citadel Press, 1963.

_____. *Economy and Society*. Guenther Roth and Claus Wittich, editors. New York: Bedminister Press, 1968.

Woll, Peter. *American Bureaucracy*. New York: Norton, 1977.

KISSINGER AND NIXON ADMINISTRATION FOREIGN POLICY

Beecher, William. "Henry the Discreet." *New York Magazine*, (April 5, 1982).

Bell, Coral. *The Diplomacy of Detente: The Kissinger Era.* New York: St. Martin's Press, 1977.

Brandon, Henry. *The Retreat of American Power.* Garden City, New York: Doubleday, 1973.

Caldwell, Dan, editor. *Henry Kissinger, His Personality and Politics.* Durham, North Carolina: Duke Press Policy Studies, 1983.

Davis, Vincent. "Henry Kissinger and Bureaucratic Politics." Institute of International Studies, Essay Series No. 9. University of South Carolina, 1979.

Fallici, Orina. *Interviews with History.* Boston: Houghton Mifflin, 1977.

Gaddis, John. *Strategies of Containment.* New York: Oxford University Press, 1982.

Graubard, Stephen R. *Kissinger: Portrait of a Mind.* New York: Norton, 1973.

Hallett, Douglas. "Kissinger Dolosus: The Domestic Politics of SALT." *The Yale Review,* Vol. LXV, No. 2 (Winter 1976).

Hersh, Seymour. *The Price of Power.* New York: Summit Books, 1983.

Hoffmann, Stanley. *Primacy or World Order.* New York: McGraw-Hill, 1978.

_____. *Dead Ends: American Foreign Policy in the New Cold War.* Cambridge, Massachusetts: Ballinger, 1983.

Joiner, Harry M. *American Foreign Policy: The Kissinger Era.* Huntsville, Alabama: Stode Publishers, 1977.

Kalb, Marvin and Bernard Kalb. *Kissinger.* New York: Dell Books, 1974.

Kissinger, Henry A. *A World Restored: Metternich, Castlereagh and the Problems of Peace 1812-1822.* Boston: Houghton Mifflin, 1957.

_____. *Nuclear Weapons and Foreign Policy.* New York: Harper, 1957.

_____. *The Necessity for Choice: Prospects for American Foreign Policy.* New York: Harper, 1961.

_____. *The Troubled Partnership.* New York: McGraw-Hill, 1965.

_____. *American Foreign Policy.* New York: Norton, 1969.

_____. *White House Years.* Boston: Little Brown, 1979.

_____. *For the Record.* Boston: Little Brown, 1981.

_____. *Years of Upheaval.* Boston: Little Brown, 1982.

_____. "The White Revolutionary: Reflections on Bismarck." *Daedalus,* Vol. 97, No. 3 (Summer 1968).

_____. "Bureaucracy and Policymaking: The Effect of Insiders and Outsiders on the Policy Process." Morton Halperin and Arnold Kanter, editors. *Readings in American Foreign Policy.* Boston: Little Brown, 1973.

Kraft, Joseph. "In Search of Kissinger." *Harper's Magazine,* Vol. 242, No. 1448 (January 1971).

Landou, David. *Kissinger: The Uses of Power*. Boston: Houghton Mifflin, 1972.

Lehman, John. *The Executive, Congress and Foreign Policy: Studies of the Nixon Administration*. New York: Praeger, 1976.

Liska, George. *Beyond Kissinger: Ways of Conservative Statecraft*. Baltimore: Johns Hopkins University Press, 1975.

Maylish, Bruce. *Kissinger: European Mind in American Policy*. New York: Basic Books, 1976.

Morris, Roger. *Uncertain Greatness: Henry Kissinger and American Foreign Policy*. New York: Harper & Row, 1977.

Newhouse, John. *Cold Dawn: The Story of SALT*. New York: Holt Rinehart, Winston, 1973.

Nixon, Richard. *RN: The Memoirs of Richard Nixon*. New York: Grosset & Dunlap, 1978.

Nutter, G. Warren. *Kissinger's Grand Design*. Washington: American Enterprise Institute, 1975.

Pett, Saul. "Henry Kissinger: Loyal Retainer or Nixon's Svengali." *Washington Post*, August 2, 1970.

Safire, William. *Before the Fall: An Inside View of the Pre-Watergate White House*. New York: Ballantine Books, 1979.

Shawcross, William. *Side-Show: Kissinger, Nixon and the Destruction of Cambodia*. New York: Simon & Schuster, 1979.

Stoessinger, John G. *Henry Kissinger: The Anguish of Power*. New York: Norton, 1976.

Szulc, Tad. *The Illusion of Peace: Foreign Policy in the Nixon Years*. New York: Viking, 1978.

Weber, William T. "Kissinger as Historian: A Historiographical Approach to Statesmanship." *World Affairs*, Vol. 141, No. 1 (Summer 1978).